Business and politics in Japan

MANCHESTER
UNIVERSITY PRESS

Business and politics in Japan

JAMES BABB

MANCHESTER UNIVERSITY PRESS
Manchester and New York

distributed exclusively in the USA by Palgrave

Copyright © James Babb 2001

The right of James Babb to be identified as the author of this work has been asserted by him in accordance with the Copyright, Designs and Patents Act 1988.

Published by Manchester University Press
Oxford Road, Manchester M13 9NR, UK
and Room 400, 175 Fifth Avenue, New York, NY 10010, USA
http://www.manchesteruniversitypress.co.uk

Distributed exclusively in the USA by
Palgrave, 175 Fifth Avenue, New York, NY 10010, USA

Distributed exclusively in Canada by
UBC Press, University of British Columbia, 2029 West Mall, Vancouver, BC, Canada V6T 1Z2

British Library Cataloguing-in-Publication Data
A catalogue record for this book is available from the British Library

Library of Congress Cataloging-in-Publication Data applied for

ISBN 0 7190 5661 6 *hardback*
     0 7190 5662 4 *paperback*

First published 2001

10 09 08 07 06 05 04 03 02 01   10 9 8 7 6 5 4 3 2 1

Typeset in Palatino with Frutiger
by Servis Filmsetting Ltd, Manchester, UK
Printed in Great Britain
by Bell & Bain Ltd, Glasgow

For Emmy, Hannah and Rei

Contents

List of tables and figures	*page*	viii
Preface		ix
List of abbreviations		xii

1 Introduction   1

I The historical and financial basis of business political involvement
2 Political business in Japan   19
3 Business and political change   36
4 The regulation of business money in politics   47

II Business and the policy-making process
5 The bureaucratic context of business politics   67
6 Political leadership and policy tribes   80
7 The changing institutional structure of business interest politics   92

III The political organisation of business
8 The politics of Keidanren   113
9 Three other key national business organisations   124
10 The politics of the organisation of industry   136
11 Social factors and the political culture of the firm   148
12 Conclusion   163

Bibliography   168
Index   173

Tables and figures

Tables

4.1	Political donations to MPs by party and source, 1998	page 58
4.2	Firms and associations donating 30 million yen or more, 1998	59
5.1	*Amakudari* destinations of former MOF officials	73
5.2	Types of semi-governmental *Amakudari* destinations in 1997	74
6.1	A 'typical' career path of a Liberal Democratic Party MP	85
6.2	*Zoku* MPs and factions in 1985	87
7.1	*Amakudari* of former officials into special public corporations	96
7.2	Changes in Japanese central government structure and cabinet posts	98
7.3	*Zoku* MPs and factions in 2000	104
7.4	Public fixed investment/GDP	108
8.1	Keidanren chairs (1948–present)	117
8.2	'Hereditary' posts in Keidanren	119
8.3	Keidanren leadership in March 2000	121
9.1	Postwar chairs of the Japan Chamber of Commerce and Industry	127
9.2	Leadership of the Keizai Doyukai (1946–present)	131
11.1	Matsushita Training Institute affiliated candidates (June 2000)	156

Figures

4.1	Political contributions in Japan (1978–99)	56

Preface

This book had many inspirations, but the bulk of the motivation for this work came from frequent conversations with Japanese businesspeople who discovered my specialism and had strong opinions on the subject. Their sincerity and the commonality of their experiences were intriguing. The issues they consistently raised led me to try to identify the patterns revealed in this book. This study was also strongly influenced by one very important business player who I very much respected. He held a key positions in the system, and though I was reluctant to pursue the issues raised while he was deeply involved, I think he would have approved of this project. In one of those unforeseen twists of fate, he died just prior to a scandal which rocked his industry and his firm, and would have probably brought him down as well. I hope to answer his questions of why the relationship between business and politics in Japan is as it is, and what can be done about it.

After finishing the manuscript I also realise my debt to my two PhD supervisors at Stanford University. The main supervisor was Professor Daniel Okimoto who has a wealth of knowledge of the inner workings of the Japanese system of political economy. At the same time, the lingering impact of Professor Philippe Schmitter informs this work. This is not as theoretical or substantive as either of these two scholars might like (and in fact I hesitate to associate either professor with this work without their permission) but it seems unfair to allow my gratitude to go unacknowledged.

While I was in Japan, I was fortunate to work for two research institutes which placed me at the centre of the business–politics relationship in Japan. I worked for over one year in the Policy Research Department of Nomura Research Institute, the largest private think tank in Japan. This gave me some important insights into a highly politicised firm. In addition, I spent three years at the National

Institute for Research Advancement (NIRA), the largest semi-governmental think tank in Japan. At NIRA, I had direct experience with many of the phenomena discussed in this book, including the complex relationship between business, bureaucracy and politicians as each were well represented and I interacted with representatives of each everyday.

My confidence to approach the subject of business also comes from experience providing business consultancy services to major firms over fifteen years. I was a consultant and, briefly President, at Interface Japan, which assisted firms in Silicon Valley, such Hewlett-Packard and Intel, in their efforts to make sense of Japan and Japanese business. In the UK, I have been a consultant for investment firms in the City of London and in Edinburgh. I have always stressed politics both inside and outside the firm as a key influence on business in Japan, and have tried to get my clients to go beyond cultural etiquette to political interests and policy context. This book hopes to help fill some of the gaps in information needed.

The patience and support of Manchester University Press has been very much appreciated in the planning and writing of this book. The research would have not been possible without the support of the Department of Politics and the Small Grants Committee of the University of Newcastle. I would also like to express my appreciation to all those who cooperated as best they could with my requests for interviews. Even those who refused did so in ways which were more helpful than they could ever imagine. Thanks go to Ms Junko Abe for help with various aspects of the project.

I always appreciate my children – Emmy, Hannah and Rei – for giving life ever more intensity and reason. It is to them I dedicate this book. Most importantly, I must thank my long-time companion, my wife Fumie, who has consistently been supportive of this and other projects.

Finally, a few technical notes:

1. Japanese names are given first name first and family name last as in normal Western order in order to avoid confusion among non-specialist readers. Every effort had been made to ensure the accuracy of names but Japanese first names in particular can have multiple readings and it has not always been possible to confirm the correct reading for more obscure business executives who are no longer active.

Preface xi

2   Japanese words are given without indication of the long vowels.
3   All translations are my own.

I take full responsibility for any inaccuracies and apologise in advance for any offence caused.

Abbreviations

GAD	General Affairs Division
GATT	General Agreement on Tariffs and Trade
GDP	gross domestic product
IT	information technology
JNR	Japanese National Railway
JR	Japan Rail
JSP	Japan Socialist Party
LDP	Liberal Democratic Party
MGA	Ministry of General Affairs
MITI	Ministry of International Trade and Industry
MOF	Ministry of Finance
MP	Member of Parliament
NGO	non-governmental organisation
NIRA	National Institute for Research Advancement
NTT	Nippon Telephone and Telegraph
OL	office lady
PARC	Political Affairs Research Committee
PM	Prime Minister
PR	public relations

1
Introduction

On 4 April 1999, in a column on economic affairs, a member of the editorial board of the conservative *Yomiuri Shimbun* newspaper in Japan pondered the changing relationship between business and politics in Japan. His starting point was that the relationship between politics and the Japanese business world (*zaikai*) often evokes the image of a secret world with its own special atmosphere. It is a place, he argued, shielded from the eyes of ordinary citizens where unknown individuals interact with one another in unknown ways: 'One could even say it is a strange fathomless pit.' Yet, in contrast to this view of the *zaikai*, he noted a recent public debate on rice market liberalisation – a deeply divisive issue in Japan – between, Ken Nagano, at the time the leader of Japan's Employers Federation, *Nikkeiren*, on the one hand, and a senior leader of the ruling Liberal Democratic Party (LDP), Koichi Kato, on the other. Nagano favoured opening market access to imported rice, given the cost of government protected rice for the employees of the companies he represented, while the conservative Kato, who is something of an agricultural policy expert, defended the rural interests which his party represented. It was not just that the two were debating publicly, but that there was real passion behind their arguments as though it really mattered. In the past, it was argued, politicians kept their disagreement behind closed doors, especially on contentious issues such as agricultural import liberalisation, and generally created secret compromises to delay dealing with the issue. This public debate was seen as heralding a change in the pattern of Japanese business involvement in politics.

This book examines the relationship between business and politics in Japan. It reviews past patterns of interaction but focuses primarily on the current state of business involvement in politics and the degree to which things have (or have not) changed. Surprisingly, there have been few studies directly addressing this subject. It has been over three decades since Chitoshi Yanaga's *Big Business and Japanese Politics* (1968) covered the subject comprehensively and only an article by Gerald Curtis in 1975 has gone anywhere near to looking at the full range of issues. Of course, there have been a number of important studies on related areas, particularly in relation to specific areas of policy making, but none makes business as a whole a central focus.

On reason for this lack of research may be that the subject is a difficult one to study. For the reasons given in the *Yomiuri* column, the relationship between business and politics in Japan is something of a black hole. Indeed, for many individuals in Japanese firms, politics is unpleasant business, and they would rather not talk about it because it is a dark murky world even for those in Japanese business themselves. It conjures up images of corruption and manipulation where firms and industries are sacrificed at the altar of political expediency. Most of those in business see politics as a nuisance, with politicians interfering in the smooth operation of the market, or tampering with the key institutional features of the economy under which they operate. This is certainly the reaction of many of those involved in business in Japan.

The premise of this book is that this is an unhealthy reaction. Business is everywhere politically embedded and it is important for those engaged in business to recognise and embrace this fact. The nature of institutional arrangements and political relationships has serious consequences for business. Nowhere is this more true than in Japan. The relationship between politics and business in Japan reveals serious problems and unresolved issues. Historically, Japanese business has been at the heart of political trends and the current debate on deregulation as a prerequisite to economic recovery has a crucial political dimension. The degree to which business and politics in Japan has changed and can change needs to be assessed.

A balanced understanding is needed, however, in order to approach these issues. This book is not disdainful of the role of business in the political system; indeed, it accepts that business must play a role in politics in a market economy. At the same time, there is little to be gained from whitewashing problems by emphasising only the positive role which business can play in politics. Instead, it is essential to confront the difficult issues head on, and to provide the tools to analyse the situation and criteria to measure change. These tools are used to provide up-to-date information on the key players, issues and trends in a changing Japan. The key political players are identified, business organisations assessed and the reach of politics into the firm revealed.

In doing so this book also provides the groundwork for a much needed reconsideration and debate of the nature of the relationship between firms and politics in Japan and elsewhere. For firms in Japan, as elsewhere, the relationship between politics and business may be murky, but this does not diminish the need for firms to engage politics constructively, nor for scholars to confront the issues creatively. Past patterns of interaction and the impact of institutional change are examined for clues as to what sorts of relationship works and what does not. These are undertaken in the chapters on political finance and the relationship of Japanese business to politics inside the firm.

The conclusions of this study are in one sense pessimistic. It will be argued that little has changed in the relationship between business and politicians in Japan despite reform initiatives and new trends in business governance. This lack of change is, in large part, due to the reluctance of business leaders and scholars to deal with the problem of the relationship between business and politics because it is difficult to research and confront. But ignoring the problem or wishing it will go away will not solve it; only a mix of increased transparency and regulation will make a healthy relationship possible.

Why is change an issue?

One might ask why is the situation undergoing change? The simple answer is chronic economic stagnation in Japan and increasing pressures for globalisation are forcing both business and the Japanese goverment to re-evaluate their relationship. Of course, globalisation is a term so vague it requires some elaboration. As Holton (1998) points out, globalisation is neither new nor should it be seen as a special challenge to Japan. Japanese business has never existed in a vacuum and, in fact, has been responsible for shaping the nature of the globalisation process itself. Indeed, the economic crisis facing Japan is largely a product of past choices made by Japan in response to previous international pressures. This is in contrast to Japan's international economic strategy and domestic political coalitions in the 1950s and 1960s which brought the country phenomenal levels of growth. It was Japan's failure to react to the changing international situation since that time that was responsible for the bubble economy of the late 1980s and early 1990s. The economic challenges of the new century are creating intense pressures on business and its relationship with the political system.

It is important to stress that Japan has always been experiencing globalisation. Japan has been a part of the international economic system since the sixteenth century. Even during the era of seculsion which lasted from the early 1600s to the mid-nineteenth century, Japan engaged in significant trade with China and had important trading relations with the Dutch. Under the uneasy balance of power between the powerful lords and the feudal Tokugawa regime, the basis of a dynamic domestic economy and skilled merchant class appeared. While lacking political power themselves, merchants established relationships with political authorities to pursue mutual gain. Even at its most isolated, Japanese business could not escape politics or the outside world.

By the end of the nineteenth century – in a key period of 'globalisation' – Japan was opening to the West, began to modernise its industry and developed a close alliance with Britain, the dominant economic and political power of the time. Japanese industrialisation was given a massive boost by Japan's participation on the side of the UK and the US in the First World War. As a result of the post-First World War settlement, which discouraged bilateral alliances, Japan was forced to sever its ties with the UK. Once Japan began to experience economic difficulties which culminated in the great depression of the 1930s, business looked to the state for protection in the form of cartels. At the same time, the military sought expansion of Japan's colonial empire – backed by significant segments of the business community, but this ended in war with the US (1941–45) and defeat. Thus, global competitive pressures have sometimes brought out a less than healthy Japanese response.

Japan's postwar success can be seen as a success for Japanese business under a US umbrella. Japan enjoyed relatively unimpeded access to the US market, US assistance in rejoining the international community (especially the GATT – General Agreement on Tariffs and Trade) and cheap raw materials (especially oil). Japan's high-growth era was made possible in part by its participation in the global economy. It is true that the US tolerated a dollar–yen exchange rate favourable to Japan (360 yen = $1) and Japanese protection of its markets, but it was always anticipated that these advantages would eventually have to go. Of course, many countries experienced similar advantages and did not have the economic success of Japan so, clearly, other factors were at work, such as private sector dynamism and the effective allocation of resources to infrastructure and growth industries. Still, the US influence should not be underestimated.

Indeed, the period of direct rule under the US-led Occupation of Japan (1945–52) was crucial to the formation of the institutional bases of the postwar firm in three key areas: labour rights, dissolution of the old economic conglomerates (*zaibatsu*) and land reform. The rights of labour to organise and form unions made possible under the Occupation created a new balance between employees and employers. Even if these rights were eroded by subsequent events through divisive strikes, company unions provided a modicum of protection to workers (especially job security) and enabled workers to strongly identify themselves with the firm. In addition, improved conditions and pay made the development of postwar consumer mass markets possible in Japan. *Zaibatsu* dissolution did not prevent prewar economic conglomerates from regrouping, but the nepotism and cronyism of the great business families of prewar Japan were replaced by self-regulating firms, run by management teams recruited from the company itself, based on seniority and merit. The new postwar groups, or *keiretsu*, were centred on interlocking ties and a strong relationship to a main bank. This made it possible for Japanese firm to take a long-term approach to markets as they were largely insulated from short-term demands for profit made by numerous stockholders. Land reform created a large class of independent farmers who supplied industry with seasonal labour but were also subsidised by the government which served as a sort of safety net. Thus, even if emphasis is placed on internal demand, a loyal workforce and the long-term view taken by Japanese firms, the US legacy still played a role.

These arrangements made possible the era of the steel and rice coalition. The State protected and promoted both steel and rice, and though there were costs to each for the benefits provided to the other, the compromise held. Businesses tolerated state inference because it also meant protection from foreign imports and promotion of its goods overseas as it learned to compete on international markets. Steel and related industries, such as automobiles, were promoted and protected but goaded into becoming internationally competitive. Politically sensitive sectors, such as agriculture, were subsided and protected more and more. Business generally saw such measures as rice price supports as necessary to maintaining a political and economic balance in

Japan which made their own success possible. In this era, open disagreements between business leaders and LDP politicians on issues such as rice import liberalisation were rare.

The problem was that Japan became more successful, it helped to contribute to the collapse of US economic hegemony and US pressures on Japan to change. In fact, the collapse of the Bretton Woods system of fixed exchange rates in the early 1970s can be directly traced to the reaction of the US to the trade challenge posed by Japan more than any other source. The US and others responded to the Japanese challenge, both politically and economically. On the political level, the US began to make increasing strident demands for more Japanese openness and responsibility towards the international system. On the economic side, US firms in the 1980s and early 1990s were compelled to restructure and either imitate or innovate in response to the Japanese challenge.

This is when the first signs of divergence of interests began to be seen in Japan. By the 1980s, business leaders would occasionally indicate a preference for progress on opening the Japanese market for agricultural goods, only to be forced to retreat in the fact of strong political pressure from farmers and their allies in the ruling LDP. The first party to opening debate agricultural import liberalisation was the Democratic Socialist Party, a minor party but composed of major manufacturing unions and closely associated with manufacturing firms. There have been complaints over the high cost of transport and telecommunications made for many years by individual business managers, but the two industries have been protected by powerful political allies and beyond debate. However, the dissension has become increasingly pronounced as the debate over rice liberalisation at the beginning of this chapter suggests. Moreover, most of the Japanese government reform scheme centres on dealing with transportation and telecommunication regulation as part of its plan to revitalise the Japanese economy. In reality, however, little progress has been made.

Indeed, Japan's reaction to political pressure from the US and other foreign competitors has often been damaging in the longrun to the Japanese economy and difficult choices have been avoided. For example, Japan used a low-interest policy to compensate for the consequences of the revaluation of the yen in the late 1980s (when the yen fell permanently below the 180 yen = \$1 level), but this policy fuelled the bubble economy and left Japanese firms burdened with debt. Business and government complicity in creating the conditions which made the bubble possible and, in many cases, corruption were part of the problem. Even after the consequences of these policies had become apparent, the Japanese government tried to delay the day of reckoning when insolvent firms would have to be allowed to fail and industries reorganised to maximise efficiency.

Now Japan searches for a new strategy in an increasingly competitive world. Even though Japan played a key role in creating many of the competitive pressures which are returning to haunt it, the record of the country in making rapid and difficult choices is not good. It carried out only grudging liberalisation in the 1970s and attempts at accommodation in the 1980s ended in the bubble economy. This time, however, it is looking to the deregulation and liberalisation strategies of others. The only choice which now seems available to Japan is to open up further and enhance competitiveness to survive. Yet, this creates conflicts not only between competitive export sectors and domestic protected sectors, but also within industries and even within firms. At every level, forces for and against change encounter a tangled web of commitments and incentives which make a clear and decisive business response impossible. Clarifying the lines of conflict and responsibility is the goal of this book.

As Weiss (1998) has argued, globalisation is mediated by internal dynamics. Like all countries, entrenched political interests shape the nature of the response. Business is embedded in relationships with the Japanese bureaucracy and with politicians, but it must also untangle itself and redefine these relationships if it is to succeed in the future. The problem is that both business leaders and politicians in Japan are confused as to how to do so. The lines separating those for and against reform are much more blurred in Japan than in the UK when Thatcher carried out economic reforms or in the US during President Reagan's initiatives in the 1980s. The problems of France and even Italy in pursuing reform are perhaps more applicable but in neither case a good match for the patterns of Japanese business–government relationships outlined below.

Nonetheless, there is a comparative dimension to the problems of Japanese business. The ways in which business articulates and fights for its interests is an issue everywhere. For example, recent debates over the need for greater regulation of political finance in advanced industrial democracies raise issues which we can fruitfully compare with the Japanese experience. Campaign finance scandals in Germany, France, the UK and the US over the past few years demonstrate that this is not a problem unique to Japan. More directly, the contradictions of corruption and growth in much of East Asia are intimately tied to problems of politics and business in the leading economy of the area, Japan.

Analysis of the business–politics relationship in Japan

The importance of Japan as a competitor and model of success or failure has meant that the relationship between business and politics in Japan has captured the attention of scholars and business leaders around the globe. Initial interest in the relationship focused on an effort to understand the reasons for Japan's phenomenal postwar economic achievements. In doing so, the notion of an 'iron triangle' between the bureaucracy, big business and the ruling party – the LDP – was used to explain how the state-led private sector dynamism created relatively high levels of economic growth in Japan until the 1990s. While the bureaucracy was given the upper hand in the relationship, business was considered to be an essential partner in the Japanese miracle. The term 'Japan Inc.' or 'Japan Plc' was coined to reflect the widespread view that the Japanese political system gave its priority to business and economic growth. Moreover, Japanese industrial policy and management philosophy was closely studied and even advocated by some Western scholars and business experts during the 1980s.

After the collapse of the economic 'bubble' in the early 1990s, however, the Japanese economy slipped into recession and the appeal of the Japanese model faded. As the consequences of the Japanese economic collapse spread, it made the economies of East Asia vulnerable to economic crisis which, in turn, worsened problems in Japan. It was only the buoyant growth of the American economy which helped to keep major Japanese exporters alive as the Japanese economy struggled to cope with overwhelming burdens of debt. Major firms such as Yamaichi Securities collapsed, and key companies such as the automobile manufacturer Nissan were compelled to seek foreign partners to remain afloat. These incidents have been duly noted by the foreign business press and have been analysed by scholars studying Japan.

In order to respond to the economic challenges facing the country, drastic institutional changes have been proposed for Japan. These reforms have sought to imitate the successful US model of deregulation and the introduction of newer, cheaper and more flexible modes of business, but they have faced considerable resistance. Many businesses that eked out a modest existence under the old system are uncertain if they will survive under the new rules. Even established firms and business organisations have been cautious in their approach to reform. More importantly, although politicians have been keen to be identified with attempts to reinvigorate the economy, they have often delayed or watered down the very proposals which would make meaningful change possible. The need to facilitate conditions for growth in the face of the challenge of the new economy is widely recognised, but it has proved difficult for the Japanese government to take swift and decisive action.

Academic scholarship focused on Japan has been relatively unhelpful in approaching these issues because it remains fixated on the second stage of consolidation and has only just begun to recognise the new pressures on Japan. A main focus of the debate is still the role of the Japanese state in the economy. The debate was started by Chalmers Johnson's *MITI and the Japanese Miracle* (1982) which argued that the powerful Ministry of International Trade and Industry (MITI) was the main force behind the Japanese miracle. Over the years several other scholars have successfully challenged the thesis that MITI alone could explain Japan's dramatic postwar economic growth. Most notable among these was *The Business of the Japanese State* (1987) by Richard Samuels which effectively argued that business in the energy sector successfully resisted state intervention at several crucial periods in the twentieth century. He argues instead for the idea of 'reciprocal consent' by which the state has authority but industry maintains control. A more recent study, focused on policies toward declining industries in Japan (Uriu, 1996), shows that domestic political factors and pressure from trading partners have constrained policy makers. Both the Samuels and Uriu studies force us to reevaluate Johnson's thesis that the postwar economy was state-led, but neither provides a detailed understanding of business interaction with politicians (so crucial to 'reciprocal consent') and the domestic factors which constrain policy making.

This consensus, however, has begun to be eroded. Not surprisingly, recent academic articles and scholarly debates recognise that something is happening but the significance is unclear (Dore, 1999; Pempel, 1998; Vogel, 1999; Yamamura, 1997). Nonetheless, there seems to be broad agreement among Japan experts on a few issues. They argue that eventually Japan will have to reform its system of regulating the economy though it will take longer than most hope or predict. Further, they suggest that the outcome of the reform process will have features peculiar to Japan even if the models and impetus for reform come from outside Japan. Finally, they seem unable to pin down the position of domestic Japanese political actors, especially business leaders and politicians, as some view their reform goals and proposals as ambiguous and problematic.

In many ways, this says nothing new because, as was noted above, there has been constant pressure for, and progress toward change as the slow rise of the influence of the competitive export sectors as a political force as is apparent in the chapters that follow. Moreover, for many years cross-cutting pressures have limited the willingness of these firms and industries to challenge the LDP, the champion of conservatism against the strong electoral threat from the left. It was only after the collapse of the left in the 1990s and the threat of the competitive weakness of Japanese firms (due to debt and competitive pressures) that has led to increased demand for change which has brought the issues to a head. It is by no means clear whether the LDP will bend to business demands, and the evidence is that they will respond fitfully and only when economic reforms can be twisted to suit LDP interests. Therefore, the first step in understanding change is to assess the nature and sources of business political power. This has not been accomplished systematically in any of the studies cited above.

Individual agents and historical trends

This study has approached the problem of the relationship between politics and business by focusing on the specific 'agents' of the relationship rather than on general structural imperatives which are often assumed to drive individual behaviour. In this sense, it follows other scholars of Japanese politics who are frequently accused of focusing too much on individuals at the expense of structural factors which might explain historical trends. Yet, even after accepting that structural factors – such as economic interests, institutions and international relationships – are important, it is individuals who act as the agents of change. Existing scholarship tends to aggregate individual business actors into 'business' as an actor, without making important distinctions between types of business players, their means and motives.

Introduction

This research starts with a review of the business–politics relationship, but makes an initial distinctions between political business (*seisho*), responsible business and policy business (*seisaku sho*). The first type (*seisho*) are entrepreneurs who use politics to expand their business interests. *Seisho* have been behind many of the major firms in Japan but some of the most recent cases of the phenomena have produced scandals which have brought down governments and profoundly shaped politicians' relationships with all businesses. Responsible leaders have tried to oppose corruption and promote reform but without success. One reason for their lack of success has been the emergence of policy business (*seisaku sho*) which exploits particular policy domains with consequences for the political economy of Japan that are as disasterous as *seisho*.

Next, a close look is taken at the policy-making process. First the powers of the bureaucracy are considered. While the influence of the bureaucracy is important, it is sometime exaggerated in studies of policy making because of bureaucratic control of the minutiae of regulation. In addition, we need to look at the political features of bureaucratic power in Japan and its impact on business. Bureaucrats are politicised in Japan and much of their influence derives from their political role. However, senior officials in government agencies are limited by the fact that they are not politicians, and lack the skills and prerogatives of political leaders.

It is best if one views the Japanese government as dominated by the imperatives of factional politics led by faction leaders who are senior politicians. While factions are simply groups of Members of Parliament (MPs) organised around a leader who bargains with other leaders for government posts, these groups have become increasingly important to the politics of the ruling LDP since its formation in 1955. As the party has dominated the government for most of the last four decades, LDP faction members have held nearly all key cabinet posts. As factional groups have became larger and more organised, they have been able to command more posts in government and more resources to reward their supporters. The biggest and most powerful factions control the selection of the prime minister who controls appointments for other posts.

This is important because individual faction members need to gain experience in governmental posts in order to advance in their careers and this has implications for the role of politicians in the policy-making process. Policy expertise is one method by which individual politicians can make themselves useful to their faction by monitoring the policy-making process and intervening to protect those interests close to the faction. If successful, these faction members will be given other posts, and increasingly important posts, so that they can advance in seniority and stature. These policy-minded politicians – the so-called *zoku* or policy tribe MPs – have come to control Japanese policy making, and the consequences of their approach to policy are crucial to understanding the business–politics relationship.

The *zoku* politicians are the ones to which firms and business associations turn to protect and extend their interests. While it would be easy to get bogged down in the minutiae of policy debate, making and implementation, it is the overall impact of *zoku* on the policy-making process which must be the focus in this study. It is only by an examination of the overall impact of a set of policies that the full implications of *zoku* politics can be made clear. A brief case study of the politics and politics which led to the bubble economy provides such an overview in a later chapter of this book. This political dimension is often hidden, missed or ignored. The new economy claims to be different but seems not to be immune from similar dynamics. This book seeks to identify actors and processes in the business–politics relationship. In particular, it identifies the current *zoku* MPs for the key economic policy domains – a list that has been updated to take into account the changes caused by the 2000 general election.

Key business players: organisational leaders and entrepreneurs

The chapters which follow the policy-making discussion similarly identify the new generation of business leaders. However, it should noted at this point that the identification of the politically involved business presents serious difficulties of research design and methodology. For example, a study of *The Business of Japanese Foreign Aid* (Soderberg, 1996) focusing on Japanese Overseas Development Assistance and based on interviews with business people, politicians, journalists, non-governmental organisations (NGOs) and academics, required considerable resources to complete the research:

> [Information] was mostly not handed out at first request but required a considerable amount of persistence and confidence-building measures. Numerous interviews were conducted off the record and many of them outside regular offices ... This implies a considerable amount of footwork from all the researchers involved. This is probably

another reason why no similar research project has been undertaken so far. It is time-consuming and requires a considerable amount of effort to collect information at the implementation level. This project could not have been undertaken by one person. What was required was a group of researchers working systematically and collecting information on a massive scale. (Ibid. 10)

In contrast, this research was conducted on a more modest scale, but overall, there is much new and substantial information.

It has been easiest to explore the political role of the major business organisations in Japan. These organisations have changed substantially over time and the patterns of leadership selection provide important clues to the political influence of particular sectors and industries. The book also examines the limits of social, regional and industrial organisation as a source of business political influence. These are often given prominence in analyses of Japanese business political power, but can be shown to be less important than usually suggested. More important is the role of industry associations. However, rather than examine one industry (as is often the case), this study looks at patterns of association with political involvement across the entire range of industries and discovers some that are useful.

The main problem in conducting the research for this book was associated with the design of the project which focused on the individual firm. The original design was based on the Hunter method used in community power studies (Hunter, 1953). In community-power studies, interviews of a community are carried out to identify key leaders who are in turn interviewed to identify other leaders until a 'map' of the community leadership structure is obtained though the overlapping results of the interviews. The plan was to interview members of firms, at the bureau chief level or above, to identify the key business leaders involved in political activities, and then systematically interview those indentified as important by others until a clear picture emerged.

Nearly 100 major firms were approached during the initial stages of the research. Understandably for this type of cold contact, the response rate was low. However, it was surprisingly low by any standard. Only five individuals were willing to participate in formal interviews and even they stressed that they spoke as individuals and not on behalf of their firms. Of course, it was anticipated that Japanese business managers would be wary of those individuals who approached them without introductions from someone they knew and respected. Therefore, a number of informal contacts were also used. Yet, it soon transpired that even willing and eager contacts were heavily discouraged from participating in interviews by their superiors. With some investigation and informal discussion, the obstacle to interviews became clear and in all cases was the same: the same key bureau chief (*bu-cho*) heading a central department in every firm, the general affairs division (*somubu*), prohibited the interviews. Since this problem relates to the internal political organisation of the firm, a full analysis will be deferred to a later chapter. It should suffice here to say that this experience created a strong impression of the distaste and fear of even a structured discussion of politics in many firms.

In any case, it soon became clear that the most politically involved members of the firm were involved with politics as a function of their position in the business or business organisations. By identifying the position in the firm, the type of firm and the post in business organisations, one can identify the main politically active members of the business community. Reputation, which is central to the Hunter methodology, rarely plays a role. This point was confirmed by further research, including less formal contact with businesses and individuals in related fields. This informal contact included correspondence and casual conversations with key individuals. That is, interviews and correspondence confirmed the fact that types of political leadership in business flow from the organisation of business, including formal business associations, informal industry leaders and the internal organisation of firms, with a more dubious role played by political business entrepreneurs and organised crime. The key political business players in Japan can be easily identified by organisational analysis. Reputation is an issue only outside the pale of institutionalised or organised business behaviour.

As a result of the reluctance of those involved in business to participate in this research, greater weight has been placed on primary and secondary source materials. Despite these limitations, the information this study uses is more extensive, goes deeper and is more up to date than other studies on business and politics in Japan. The main sources of business power are looked at extensively and important distinctions are made between types of firms, industries and industry associations. In addition, the internal politics of the firms is laid bare for the first time.

At the end of this book, the final chapter examines the problems

Introduction

of establishing a healthy relationship between firms and politicians in Japan. It concludes that there are conflicting views on the nature of the relationship between politics and the firms, which suggest conflicting options.

These views are paralleled by the main approaches taken in democracies with market economies: one focused on transparency and the other on regulation. The successes of, and prospects for, both approaches are assessed in the Japanese context in light of the dynamics of the relationship between business and politics outlined in this book.

Part I

The historical and financial basis of business political involvement

2
Political business in Japan

Key business players have been political throughout Japanese history, and this includes an important role in some of the dramatic changes in recent years. This chapter will approach the political impact of business by focusing on business interests. Admittedly, it is difficult to specify a general business interest, due to conflicting sectoral dynamics and priorities, so instead one must look at the divergent and sometimes convergent interests of the key business players. It is possible to reveal an overall pattern of the relationship between the state and business interests. However, a distinction between three types of business actors will be noted. One focus is on mainstream business leaders who can be very critical of the practices of leading politicians at key junctures and attempt to have a political impact. A second type of interaction is policy business or *seisaku sho* wherein business cooperates with government policy initiatives for mutual gain. Finally, a very important role is also played by what one could describe as political business or *seisho* which exists in the murkiest corners of the relationship between politics and business. The biggest problem in Japan is that it is often difficult to distinguish clearly between these three types because all tend to interact together and even cooperate with one another.

This problem of untangling business interests and politics is not unique to Japan. As Graham Wilson pointed out in his respected *Business and Politics*:

> politics and business can vary both within the same country over time, and between different capitalist countries at the same time. The degree to which business is organised politically; the attitudes of the public to business; links between different interests and political parties; the degree to which there are institutionalised ties between business and goverment; and the degree to which business faces the

hostility of organised interests against it all vary from place to place and time to time. (Wilson, 1990: 37)

Many of these issues will be addressed in later chapters, but the central theme of this chapter is the broad historical trend in the relationship between business interests and political parties or politicians.

There is never going to be a tight correlation between interests, parties and politicians because of cross-cutting cleavages and the eccentricities of individual businesspeople and politicians. Nonetheless, one can identify the main cleavages which influence political divisions. There has been a continuing tension in Japan between light industry (such as textiles) and heavy industry (steel, chemicals, machinery, etc.). In recent years, a serious cleavage has developed between internationally competitive exporters and domestic protected sectors. There has also been a consistent split between the politically connected versus politically 'clean', and a connected fissure between the regulated and those who want to remove regulation for their own interests.

As the last of these divisions indicates, the degree to which business interests are institutionalised is important. Political business types often emerge when the regulatory institutions have either collapsed or are in the process of institutional/economic transition. This is not unique, as a cursory glance at the former socialist economies would quickly suggest. Periods of institutional change, both political and economic, create opportunities for political business entepreneurs because new institutional rules are weak or uncertain. In contrast, the business establishment often has the advantage of defending existing institutional arrangements and shaping new rules at the highest level of government. Yet, even for the establishment, a knowledge of and involvement in the political process are seen as essential. While business leaders who represent established interests are clearly different from the political entrepreneurs engaged in *seisho*, both aim to enhance their business interests through political involvement. Moreover, many established firms have continued to be caught engaging in dubious practices even if *seisho* are more prominent in their excesses. The best that can be said is that the more institutionalised nature of established business makes them appear more politically responsible. In a sense, all business is political business.

The political origins of the Japanese business elite

When the feudal regime headed by the Tokugawa family since the early sixteenth century began to collapse in the mid-nineteenth century, those who sought to replace the decaying order turned to entrepreneurs for assistance. The leaders of the *coup d'etat* which overthrew the Tokugawa regime and placed the emperor, Meiji, on the throne in 1868 received help from a number of business entrepreneurs who were to gain financially under the new Meiji regime. Morikawa (1992) identified five such enterprenuers, which he termed 'political merchants' (*seisho*) which I render as political business. These five businesses became the majority of the powerful economic conglomerates (*zaibatsu*) which dominated the Japanese economy before 1945.

The only one of these five with roots that predate the Meiji Restoration was the House of Mitsui. Mitsui began as a kimono maker and used its success to enter into financial services. Yet, Mitsui is one of the oldest leading firms in Japan today because of its political choices and not the strength of its traditions. Indeed, there were many businesses in the Tokugawa era as successful as Mitsui if not more so, but what distinguished Mitsui from the rest was it connections with government. Even under the Tokugawa regime, Mitsui had lent money to the struggling government but soon was able to take control of the lucrative business of collecting customs and import duties for the government in the ports of Edo (Tokyo) and Yokohama, newly opened to commerce with the West. However, Mitsui was also astute enough to take a risk on backing the leaders of the coup which overthrew the Tokugawa regime, and after the coup the new government allowed them to continue their privileged relationship with the government. Other major firms which stood steadfastly with the Tokugawa regime collapsed or declined.

The remaining four *seisho* which evolved into *zaibatsu* were Yasuda, Okura, Fujita and Mitsubishi. The most significant of these four is Mitsubishi. The founder of Mitsubishi was Yataro Iwasaki, a low-status samurai in the Tosa domain. Under the Tokugawa regime, the country was divided into domains (*han*) and samurai were essentially the civil servants serving the lord (*daimyo*) of the domain. While better known for their policing functions, samurai were engaged in all aspects of administration. Iwasaki was appointed to an industry promotion branch of the Tosa in the port city of Nakasaki in another domain, and also dealt with merchants in the main commercial centre of Tokugawa Japan in Osaka. After domains were abolished in the Meiji Restoration, Iwasaki assumed some of the assets, including two steamships, and part of the debts of the former Tosa domain in a effort to set up an independent business. He received a commission to provide transportation to a Japanese military expedition in 1874. While the Meiji state had supported a rival firm as its main source of sea transport, it dissolved in 1875 and the Mitsubishi Steamship Company controlled the very profitable business of providing government naval transport in war and peace. (Morikawa, 1992: 12–15)

Mitsui and Mitsubushi are important because they were the main sponsors to the two largest political parties in prewar Japan, though one should point out they represented slightly different interests. Mitsui was the older Tokugawa retailer which stuck closer to traditional industries such as commerce, financial services, textiles and mining. Mitsubishi was much more of an industrial concern than Mitsui, with a greater emphasis on heavy and chemical industries. Mitsui backed the prewar party, the Seiyukai (Association of Political Friends), one of the oldest Japanese political parties. The Seiyukai was dominated by landlords, traditional manufacturers and members of the old financial and commercial establishment. Mitsubishi, in contrast, backed the newer and more progressive party, the Minseito, which grew out of a movement in the early 1920s to establish party government and expanded suffrage. While the Minseito also had its share of traditional landlords and members of the old commercial establishment who blocked progressive political change, it also included manufacturers and others who favoured political and social reform.

The problem for prewar parties is that they were too corrupt and too weak to pursue effective change. They appeared to be corrupt precisely because of their dependence on big business. Moreover, politicians' use of business funds and government largesse to secure re-election undermined the fragile image of prewar democracy. At the same time, the parties never had full control of the government. In theory the emperor was sovereign and those with direct access to the emperor – such as the Privy Councillor and the War Minister – effectively spoke on the emperor's behalf. These non-elected officials often used their powers to curtail the control of parties over government. When military radicals began to attack the political parties and their connections with big business, the non-elected officials gradually squeezed politicians out of office. Within one year after Japan declared war on the US in December 1941, business was put under a tight military regime of economic controls.

During the war Japanese industry faced military and bureaucratic interference with its operations, and many firms attempted to resist the ruinous demands of the wartime state (Samuels, 1987). Even so, business gained in many ways as a result of the war. While light industry, particularly textiles, may have suffered as looms were dismantled and factories converted to wartime production, the war effort gave a boost to the development of heavy industry, including the steel, chemical and machinery industries central to postwar Japanese industrial success. Firms benefited from subsidies from the state and from the development of a large industrial workforce skilled in advanced industrial techniques. Moreover, postwar strategic bombing surveys found that the air war had destroyed factories but often equipment and materials were relatively undamaged.

The war also heralded the emergence of new entrepreneurs and new industrial concerns. The Nakajima concern centred around the Nakajima Aircraft Company was one such new conglomerate, and one with a significant involvement with political parties. Nakajima, however, supported the politicians closest to the wartime regime and suffered the most as a result of the end of the war. Similarly, the Nissan concern also grew as a result of its war contract but then largely collapsed after the war leaving behind only a handful of viable firms, including Nissan Automobiles. New businesspeople also emerged on a smaller scale, such as the father of Keizo Obuchi (Prime Minister 1998–2000). Like many of those who benefited from the war, Obuchi's father ran for a seat in the postwar parliament.

After defeat in 1945 Japan was occupied by the Allied Powers (US, UK and the Commonwealth, China and Russia) which systematically sought to dissolve the *zaibatsu* which they blamed for holding back social progress in Japan and supporting the war effort. While the family-controlled stockholding companies which dominated the *zaibatsu* were dissolved and their shares sold to the public to democratise industry, the removal of family control also allowed a new class of business professionals to take control of firms.

Institutional collapse also led to the emergence of a vigorous black market in Japan at which time right-wing politicians and gangsters became closely involved with each other in Japan at both the local and national level (Kaplan and Dubro, 1986). Even after the end of the black market, these relations continued and became a fact of political and business life in Japan. The funding of political parties in the immediate postwar period was said to be highly reliant on black marketeers for political finance. For example, Kakuei Tanaka, the owner of a construction company who ran successfully for parliament in the years immediately after the war, is alleged to have used the black-market money to finance his campaigns and that of others. Moreover, he maintained ties to businesspeople with a similar background, such as Kenji Osano, throughout the postwar period. Osano and other associates of politicians from this period are often referred to as the postwar *seisho* given their use of political connections for business gain.

At the same time, the growth of heavy industry during the war also widened the split in the Japanese economy between the traditional sector and the more modern industrial sector. The politics of industrial policy were a major issue in the immediate postwar period, and state predominance during the war and its immediate aftermath gave the edge to heavy industry. Samuels (1987) is correct that business successfully resisted heavy-handed approaches of the wartime regime and that a large degree of complicity was required for the postwar heavy industry drive to succeed. Indeed, the acquiescence of business was sought to such an extent that the notion of the autonomy of the state can be questioned. However, it would not be wrong to view the state–heavy industry alliance as more of a coalition (or as in Samuels' 'reciprocal consent'). This is the heyday of Japanese industrial policy as described by Johnson's (1982) *MITI and the Japanese Miracle*. The state had the tools to force business compliance; but there were also businesses with interests which met with the goals of the bureaucracy.

Business and the creation of the LDP

There was also a political dimension to this struggle to promote modern industry in Japan. The differing industrial interests in the 1950s championed different political parties, namely the Liberal Party and the Democratic Party. Liberal Party leaders tended to have strong connections with light industry and the financial elite, while the Democratic Party tended to be backed by heavy industries, particularly those associated with defence. The policy orientations of the two parties reinforced these associations. In particular, the bureaucracy –

encouraged by like-minded politicians – sought to wind down light industries such as textiles and build up heavy industry such as automobiles, steel and chemicals. In the end, the Liberal Party was fighting a losing battle and the Democratic Party was growing stronger.

The merger of the two parties into the Liberal Democratic Party in 1955 was a direct consequence of overwhelming business pressure. The merger avoided a showdown between industrial sectors by combining both interests into one party. In addition, the Socialists had already merged into one party in 1955, and many senior business leaders were eager for the conservatives achieve unity in the face of the Socialist challenge.

Despite the merger, earlier patterns of business associations continued with individual politicians. When Kishi became Prime Minister (1958–60), for example, he maintained business connections among his classmates at Tokyo University, colleagues from the days he spent in building up the industries of Japanese-occupied Manchuria (1905–45) and the industries he worked with as wartime Minister of Munitions (Hara, 1995: 237). Steel companies were an important source of support for Kishi as well as the Sumitomo group of industries (Iyasu, 1984: 107). His strong advocacy of Japanese rearmament reinforced the heavy industry bias. In contrast, Kishi successor Ikeda (Prime Minister 1960–65) was a former Finance Ministry bureaucrat and direct heir to the Liberal Party with strong connections with the financial services sector, especially brokerage houses, and light industry (Tadamiya, 1963: 229).

Another important feature of this period was that Japanese business was provided with a large measure of protection from foreign competition by restrictions on access to the Japanese market. While many Japanese firms are internationally competitive and vigorously favour free trade, this was not the case before the 1970s. This is also reflected in the residual attempts by MITI to avoid serious liberalisation as outlined by Johnson (1982). Politicians willingly joined in the effort to avoid opening the Japanese market, especially when the pressures for liberalisation were directed at core constituencies, such as textiles.

Even as attempts where made to liberalise, most industries continued to be regulated by the government in some form. Permits were needed to establish many types of business and even to expand the business through the creation of new branches and factories. Sometimes the bureaucracy could be heavy-handed, so in key situations, business learned to rely on politicians to intervene on their behalf with the bureaucracy. A dramatic example occurred in 1965, when LDP Finance Minister, Kakuei Tanaka, ordered the bureaucracy to save Yamaichi Securities from collapse over the objections of senior officials. Such intervention became the centrepiece of the day-to-day relationship between politicians and business. Therefore, even though most firms benefited in some way from the postwar institutional framework, the LDP was useful to the protection of their interests and they gave political donations to the LDP accordingly.

The early 1960s was also the period of the four 'kings of business' and perhaps the peak of informal business influence (Nihon Keizai Shimbun Sha, 1990: 205; Tahara, 1986: 45–68). The four were Ataru Kobayashi (first president of the Japan Development Bank), Naruo Mizuno (president of Sankei Shimbun), Shigeo Mizuno (president of Fuji Steel) and Takeshi Sakurada (president of Nissin Textiles). While these individuals represented a range of industries, they were not the leaders of any of the top business organisations nor were they from the former *zaibatsu*. Their power derived entirely from their close personal relationship with Prime Minister Ikeda and their widespread connections across the parochial divides of the business community. The most dramatic manifestation of their influence came when Ikeda fell ill and was choosing his successor. Ikeda initially favoured the faction boss Ichiro Kono, but the four opposed Kono and persuaded Ikeda to support the former bureaucrat Eisaku Sato instead. It has been suggested that the reason they opposed Kono was that he had his own independent sources of money, some of it of dubious origin, and therefore he was not dependent on business community funding and would not be sensitive to their wishes (Tahara, 1986: 68–70).

Sato (Prime Minister 1965–72), in contrast, maintained relations with the types of business favoured by Kishi, in part because connections bequeathed to him by his brother Kishi, and in part due to relatively pro-military credentials from his days as a bureaucrat in the prewar and wartime Transport Ministry. At the same time, Sato was also a former Liberal Party leader and educated at the prestigious Tokyo University so he maintained good relations with a range of industries, though his 'hawkish' inclinations still attracted more support from heavy industry, especially those with defence production connections. All forms of business seemed to converge in support of the LDP under Sato. In fact, by the late 1960s divergent interests were masked as time passed since the LDP merger, in part due to high levels of economic growth, but primarily because all faction leaders began to diversify their sources of financial support.

Regardless of how seriously one takes the myth of the four kings of business, their influence waned by the end of the 1960s. Instead, the business political influence became regularised into the organisations which represent business. Indeed, two of the four kings, Shigeo Mizuno and Takeshi Sakurada, became the heads of the Japan Chamber of Commerce and Industry and the Japanese Employers Association respectively. Yet, overall it was the Federation of Business Organisations, Keidanren, that began to speak as the authoritative voice of business in politics. Keidanren had been founded in 1946 but it was under Kogoro Uemura, chair from 1968 to 1974, that the group became more organised and effective as a political force. Ironically, however, Uemura was a former civil servant and not a businessman even though he was called the 'prime minister of the business community'.

Even at this point, however, business influence was indirect because few businesspeople became politicians. Indeed, there was only one clear LDP faction leader with an established business background at this time, Aiichiro Fujiyama, former President of the Japan Chambers of Commerce and Industry. However, it is notable that Fujiyama was not more successful as a faction leader despite the fact that he came directly from the business community. In fact, it has been argued that Fujiyama's lack of success was precisely because he was from the business community so was reluctant to go and beg industry for funds (Tahara, 1986: 69). Therefore, after two unsuccessful bids for the leadership of the LDP, Fujiyama lost out to a new breed of unscrupulous politicians who had diverse if sometimes dubious sources of money. In any case, a direct business representative was not needed because the LDP was the party of business, especially given the threat posed by a growing left-wing opposition, so business placed the success and unity of the LDP as its highest priority.

Political competition, policy and corruption

The impact of this new breed of unscrupulous politicians became clear when one such politician – Kakuei Tanaka, mentioned above – rose to succeed Sato as Prime Minister in 1972. Tanaka was a rare former businessman among the former bureaucrats of the LDP leadership, but unlike Fujiyama he had been an outsider in the business establishment and entered politics directly at the local level after his brief business success during the war. Given his humble origins and lack of bureaucratic or other central government connections, Tanaka had to be especially creative in exploiting any possible sources of money. He did so by establishing a reputation for getting things done, as in the Yamaichi Securities bail-out. At the same time, he was suspected of making possible the sale of government lands on favourable terms to a business associate. By acting on behalf of both established firms and entrepreneurs willing to manipulate the political system, Tanaka built a strong financial base.

Competition for funds became particularly intense during the fight to succeed Sato as Prime Minister which was fought between Tanaka and his main rival Takeo Fukuda. Fukuda was the opposite of Tanaka. Fukuda had been educated at the elite Tokyo University, worked as a bureaucrat in the powerful Ministry of Finance (MOF), and was the candidate supported by Japan's business establishment. The flow of funds to LDP MPs to persuade them to support one or the other of the candidates was unprecedented. Both sides were heavily financed by business sources, though on balance Tanaka seems to have depended less on established business and business organisations.

Indeed, Tanaka was initially opposed by the business establishment who favoured the former MOF bureaucrat Fukuda. Once in power, however, the business community grudgingly accepted Tanaka. In some respects, Tanaka was very good for business. He had come to power on a platform of a radical redevelopment of Japan which involved a decentralisation of industry away from major cities such as Tokyo to less developed rural areas of Japan. The rural areas also happened to be the key support base of the LDP and the massive public commitment to infrastructure improvements provided unbelievable opportunities for gain on the part of construction companies and real estate speculators who purchased potential sites where industry might be relocated. Established firms, too, could benefit from the improved infrastructure and incentives to develop greenfield sites in rural areas.

This is why the business community agreed to help the LDP in the 1974 Upper House election. There was a real fear that the left would win and any potentially successful candidates were welcomed. While many in the business community were sceptical at first, a number of firms willingly sponsored candidates, in particular the firms of the Hitachi and Mitsubishi groups of companies. The attempt to use corporations for political purposes faced a groundswell of criticism, especially when large amounts of money seemed to have been used in potential violation of campaign restrictions, and when employees and suppliers complained at being forced to support the company's candidate. In the end, most of these candidacies were unsuccessful, with the Mitsubishi candidate going down to defeat along with candidates supported by Japan Steel, Kawasaki Steel, Idemitsu Petroleum and Toshiba. However, the Hitachi candidate won largely because she was a popular former actress with a base of support which predated the support of the company (Blaker, 1976; 65–70). Nonetheless, the LDP narrowly escaped defeat.

Unfortunately for Tanaka, this was not the end of his problems but the beginning. His massive government spending plans ran into trouble almost immediately as a result of the first oil crisis and the breakdown of the Bretton Woods system of fixed exchange rates. Japan's skyrocketing land prices took off in this period. Moreover, Tanaka's dubious fundraising practices began to be exposed in the press and internal opposition in the LDP forced him to resign. Tanaka was further discredited after leaving office when he was indicted and convicted of bribery in the Lockheed scandal, where he agreed to intervene on behalf of the Lockheed corporation in the purchase of aeroplanes for the Japanese government.

Responsible types: Doko and Matsushita

Tanaka's administration heralded the beginning of the end of the close relationship between the LDP and business. One of the first businessmen to oppose Tanaka while he was still in office was the leader of Keidanren, Toshio Doko (former chair of Tokyo Electric Company), who even suggested that organised business funding of politicians, such as that carried out by Keidanren, should stop altogether. His call for an end to contributions to the LDP was echoed by other major business leaders (Tahara, 1986: 118–25). Tanaka's resignation put an end to the notion of a cut-off of political funding, and no more progress was made in large part because other mainstream business leaders thought that Doko and the others were naive to believe business could ignore the LDP.

Several years later, however, a second challenge by an established business leader also came as an indirect result of Tanaka. The end of the Tanaka administration was not just due to scandal. It was also caused by international economic forces associated with the collapse of the Bretton Woods system of fixed exchange rates, inflation caused by Tanaka's spending programmes and the first and second oil crises (1973 and 1978). As the level of economic growth fell in Japan, the Japanese government budget deficit grew massively. Moreover, large firms began to move some production overseas and had to find cost savings at home in order to maintain competitiveness. Finally, it was necessary to avoid trade friction with Japan's largest market: the US. This meant that Japan had to deregulate and open up its internal market at least to an extent necessary to appease the US.

As fiscal crisis and outside pressure for deregulation intensified from the 1970s onward, it revealed underlying political tensions within Japan between conflicting economic interests. Even though the push for deregulation is often identified with foreign, primarily US, government pressures to open the economy to foreign competition, competitive firms within Japan also became more eager to remove restrictions when opportunities for gain seemed to be available. A few maverick firms, in particular, have been able to achieve success without the protection of a major group or licensing protection or favourable allocation of resources. Finally, successful export firms have not always hidden their willingness to sacrifice protection of less competitive sectors in order to maintain free trade.

The most active attempt by a major business leader to force a change in LDP dominance was Konosuke Matsushita's bid to create a new party by splitting the LDP in the early 1980s (Yamaguchi, 1983). In the end, the plan foundered on the divergent interests of the individual companies in the Matsushita group (including such brands as National and Panasonic) as well as a lack of support from other exporters. Nonetheless, Matsushita did elect a handful of MPs, mostly former researchers from his PHP Research Institute, who joined the LDP (Itagaki, 1987: 75–89). The firm has recently tried to emerge from the shadow of the Matsushita legacy, but the Matsushita's executive training institute, Matsushita Juku, still produces the largest number of business candidates who successfully run for parliamentary seats.

The main reason why other firms would not join the Matsushita crusade is that they realised that the management of pressures for deregulation and openness had the troubling political implications for business in Japan. The electoral decline of the LDP and the growth of the left-wing opposition in the 1970s led business to be very careful

Political business in Japan

not to undermine the LDP. Thus, policies that were protective of the rural heartland of the LDP were tolerated, especially the protection of agriculture and the retail industry, and policies aimed at the provision of government largesse to rural communities were even encouraged and enjoyed by business. That is, even the so-called responsible business interests were deeply enmeshed in an institutional environment based on policies which benefited them as well as those they complained about.

Policy business (*seisaku sho*)

This deep involvement of even established business with the murkier side of Japan comes through business involvement in the policy process. Politicians have the power to create policy domains in which government contracts and programmes provided profitable opportunities covering a large range of economic interests including those represented by Japan's major industrial groups. The politics of creating these opportunities, through the manipulation of existing or development of new government programmes has also led to a new type of politically involved business, policy business (*seisaku sho*).

The origin of policy business was an intensification of fundraising activities by the major LDP factions to compete or even survive as Japan entered the 1980s. The previous pattern of the dependence of a faction leader on one set of industries or individual business sponsors was supplemented with a wider base of companies and individuals. In part, these new sources of support were cultivated by a new form of interest politics which like Tanaka's ambitious plans to restructure Japan, relied on massive government initiatives. Business benefited and rewarded politicians for creating the opportunities.

During the Nakasone administration, the head of Mitsubishi Research Institute was put in charge of Nakasone's Economic Policy Research Group to utilise private enterprise partnerships to reduce the cost of public works to the Japanese government. The work of the group identified several areas in which private enterprise might supplement government spending to the benefit of the private sectors as well. It should not be surprising that, of the areas identified, the development of the new Kansai international airport directly benefited the Mitsubishi group of companies which had helped the Group's research (Saito, 1985: 90–120).

This was not unique. For most faction leaders and their related

MPs, there were a range of policies – primarily focused on economic development, especially rural and/or regional development, and the related industries of (construction, real estate, etc.) – which might lead to lucrative policy initiatives. Even in industries such as electronics seemingly unrelated to public works, special government-funded projects could provide a valuable market for goods for which internal demand was weak or economies of scale were difficult to achieve. For example, government procurement of computers or other electronics industries products for schools and other public facilities boosted the sales of firms which produced economic products which did not have the market demand of the consumer electronics of Matsushita (Panasonic), Sony and other successful Japanese corporations of the 1980s.

These arrangements tended to benefit existing firms, both the old economic conglomerates, such as Mitsubishi, and the firms favoured by the government, such as Japan Steel and the NTT family of companies. Export firms, particularly in the consumer electronics and automobile industries, also benefited directly and indirectly from domestic consumption in Japan. However, other firms were outside of the cosy relationship. This was especially true of highly ambitious entepreneurs who continued to try to carve out a niche in Japan's highly competitive service industries. Some of these individuals engaged in old-fashioned political business (*seisho*) tactics in order to grow.

Political parvenus: the new *seisho*

Two cases of *seisho* – involving Recruit and Sagawa Express companies – need to be examined because they have had a profound influence on the laws governing the relationship between politicians and business. Their story suggests that the concept of *seisho* is not something which can be dismissed as a past phenomenon or replaced by *seisaku sho* because recent developments in Japanese politics can be traced to the scandals caused by these political parvenus acting as new *seisho*. Moreover, these problems are related to the current problems of deregulation in Japan. When asked whether deregulation would decrease the incidence of scandal in Japan, an official with Keidanren argued that it was deregulation which made possible the Recruit and Sagawa scandals (Keidanren interview). The implication was that deregulation is more likely to produce the conditions in which the new *seisho* can flourish.

The scandals emerged from very different industries. Recruit was a publisher of a wide variety of magazines and dabbled in other service business, and Sagawa was an express delivery company. Recruit flourished in the 1980s because a large workforce, and in particular working women, had disposable income, and a variety of magazines, leisure services and goods were produced to cater to this growing market of young women, especially the ubiquitous office lady (OL). In fact, young people in general could more easily find lucrative short-term employment and had more to spend, and it was at this market that the Recruit corporation's magazines, ranging from job announcements to travel, were targeted and this explains why Recruit had become so rich so fast.

The president of Recruit sought information and influence wherever he could buy it. He made generous donations to leading politicians – primarily through the purchase of tickets to political receptions – and provided loans to them as well. However, another side to Ezoe's political activities was revealed when he was arrested on 13 February 1989. Recruit had also used its money to buying sensitive or privileged information from governmental agencies and used it to influence and tamper with government procurement. As a result, others in the bureaucracy or governmental corporations were also arrested. On 6 March, Hisashi Shinto, the Chair of Nippon Telephone and Telegraph (NTT), Japan's main telecommunications company, was arrested as part of the Recruit scandal. The same month a former administrative vice-minister from the Labour Ministry, Hiroshi Kato, and another from the Education Ministry, Kunio Takaishi were also arrested in connection with the Recruit scandal.

There were also suspicions that donations to politicians meant that they were also somehow involved. Eventually, Prime Minister Takeshita's government had to admit on 11 April in the Lower House Budget Committee that Takeshita's parliamentary secretary and others received 151 million yen from the Recruit Corporation as a political donation in the form of party ticket sales. While he insisted that this was the full extent of the monies from Recruit, on 22 April, the *Asahi Shimbun* newspaper reported that Takeshita's secretary borrowed 50 million yen from Recruit in 1987 when Takeshita was prime minister, though this money was subsequently repaid. As a result of his dishonesty and the widening scandal, Takeshita was forced to announce his resignation on 25 April 1989.

The problem for Japan was that all the top leaders of the LDP were implicated in the scandal. Temporarily a weak leader was put in place, but the result was that the 1989 Upper House election led to an overwhelming victory for the Japan Socialist Party (JSP) at the expense of the LDP. Moreover, every single one of the candidates put up by the Japan Trade Union Congress (Rengo) was elected, often with huge majorities. It was the first time the opposition had captured control of the Upper House since the formation of the LDP in 1955. Fortunately for the LDP, the Upper House is less important than the Lower House and a general election for the Lower House in early 1990 allowed the LDP to retain its majority and control of the government. However, two years later, the LDP was again embroiled in scandal with more significant consequences.

The second scandal in 1992, involving the Sagawa Express Delivery Company, had even more far-reaching implications for the relationship between politics and business in Japan. This scandal began with the need of Noboru Takeshita to secure the approval of his predecessor, Nakasone, in order to smooth his way to the premiership in 1987. Nakasone was not averse to supporting Takeshita. However, he wanted Takeshita to appease a right-wing splinter group, the Imperial People's Party (Kominto). In order to comply with Nakasone's request, Takeshita felt compelled to seek the help of Ishii Susumu, the former leader of Japan's second largest criminal syndicate. Ishii maintained connection with the extreme right and it was hoped he could persuade the group to halt its campaign. The contact person for the meeting with Ishii was Hiroyasu Watanabe, the president of the Sagawa Express Delivery Company's Tokyo subsidiary. Watanabe was eager to expand his company's share of business using Takeshita links with business and so offered to act as a go-between.

After talking to Oshima Ryumin, leader of the Kominto, Watanabe held a meeting in a Tokyo hotel with Takeshita and two of his colleagues, Shin Kanemaru and Ichiro Ozawa, at which time Takeshita agreed to publicly apologise to Tanaka for seizing control of Tanaka's faction earlier in 1987. This seemed to satisfy Oshima and the Kominto, so the right-wing campaign stopped. In exchange for his assistance, the crime syndicate chief got $2 billion in loans from Watanabe, most of which was speculated on the stock market but some of which went to the right-wing Oshima. In addition, Sagawa's Express Delivery Company suddenly received increased business from Kanemaru's network of supporters in construction and related industries. The growth of Sagawa business in Kanemaru's home turf in Yamanashi prefecture was viewed by delivery firm rivals with particular alarm. In any case, the connection served all parties well. Nakasone threw his support behind Takeshita and Takeshita became Prime Minister on 6 November 1987. The Sagawa delivery business flourished. The problem was that senior LDP politicians relied on organised crime, right-wing groups, and corrupt deals with business to smooth their rise to power.

Conclusions: business players and business interests

This chapter was intended to highlight the trends in private gain sought by political business and contrast it to the public interest rhetoric of responsible business leaders. However, it also revealed the key to both types of politically involved business: the combination of interests and organisation position in relation to political power. It expresses a range of business involvement in politics from secret deals to financial support and sponsorship of candidates to open criticism.

Big business has supported political parties, particular the LDP, because it promoted and protected business interests. Many major firms in Japan began as *seisho* and it is a strategy which still attracts interest. *Seisaku sho* is just the respectable extension of this strategy. Japanese businesspeople implicitly recognise the political basis of business in Japan However, *seisho* tactics also have political consequences, which will be discussed in the next chapter and contrasted with the relative inability of established business interests to have a sustained political impact.

3
Business and political change

The previous chapter made the distinction between *seisho* and responsible business. However, *seisho* scandal always seems to have more of a political impact than the ineffectual attempts of respectable business leaders to promote political reform. This chapter examines the political consequences of the Recruit and Sagawa scandals. In doing so, it identifies change in relationship between the ruling LDP and the business community since 1993. It was in 1993 that business mustered the courage to confront the LDP and contributed to the fall of the party from power. However, the business community was forced to accept the dominance of the LDP once it returned to power only one year later. Nearly a decade later, the new relationship is still unsettled and will never be as close as it once was. This chapter examines how this distance was created.

Business and the fall of the LDP

The Recruit and Sagawa scandals marked a shift in the relationship between business and the LDP in that business became alienated from the LDP, effectively abandoned the party and contributed to its fall from power in 1993. While public revulsion at LDP corrupt practices, such as those seen in the Recruit scandal, led to punishment of the party at the polls, this anger was usually short-lived. It was unfortunate for the LDP then that an Upper House election in the summer of 1989 provided an opportunity for the voters to express their dissatisfaction with the LDP over this and other issues. The result was that the LDP lost control of the Upper House for the first time since the formation of the party in 1955.

With a more important Lower House election looming in 1990, the LDP worried that major businesses had become ambivalent

Business and political change

toward the party and was particularly angered by the role business seemed to have played in the party's crushing defeat in the 1989 Upper House election. Only two days after the election, on the evening of 25 July, senior members of the LDP met with leaders from the Japanese automobile industry. The LDP MITI Minister, Seiroku Kajiyama, denounced the industry's leaders for their lack of support (Mainichi Shimbun, 1991: 19–20).

Kajiyama turned to Toyota Automobiles Chair Soichiro Toyota and pointed out that the company had paid for commercials during the popular evening new programme *News Station* presented by Goro Kume who frequently expressed doubts about the LDP and addressed controversial issues which were damaging to the party. The representative from Nissan was also questioned by Kajiyama over Nissan Chair Takeshi Ishihara's unprecedented demand for Takeshita's resignation earlier in the year. The situation was exacerbated by the fact that the automobile workers' unions were a key support base for the new Rengo labour federation and the companies tended to work closely with the unions in support of elements of the moderate left in order to keep the unions from the militant left. As a result, the success of the Rengo-supported candidates in the Upper House election was blamed by the LDP on automobile industry cooperation with their labour unions (ibid. 21–22). Kajiyama made it clear he was dissatisfied with business support for the LDP.

Therefore, the LDP sought more enthusiastic assistance in a counter-attack on the opposition at a meeting on 21 September when LDP General Secretary Ozawa met the chair, Eishiro Saito, and other top officials of Keidanren, Japan's main business organisation. Ozawa informed him that 2–3 hundred trillion yen would be needed for the upcoming Lower House election (ibid. 60–1). Saito was surprised at the amount being demanded which was many times the amount the LDP usually spent. Ozawa explained that individual politicians and factions had been raising money but it was not enough and the party had to take charge and raise additional funds. Saito responded by articulating growing business community doubts about the dubious manner by which donated political funds were accounted for by the LDP. After a cursory response to these concerns, Ozawa produced a list of the subsidiaries of the major firms supporting the Keidanren, which might make direct donations to the LDP. Ozawa argued, in a dramatic change to existing practice, that not only the main firm in each industry should provide the full amount of political funds permitted by law but also that each of the suppliers and subsidiaries of the firms should do so as well.

At the time, Saito appeared to agree to help if the LDP pursued effective political reform, but his response was really only aimed at avoiding a direct answer. In fact, the secretariat of Keidanren, responsible for organising political donations, resisted Ozawa's proposal by arguing that variations in cash flow, assets and profits of the various firms in an industrial group made it impossible to request fixed amounts from every major subsidiary in each of Japan's major corporate groups. Ozawa persisted by approaching each industrial federation which supported Keidanren, but also without success. Eventually, in the weeks just prior to the election, a loan was advanced to the LDP in an amount equivalent to three years' political funding guaranteed by Keidanren and paid out by Japan's major banks.

Obviously, business was growing apart from the LDP but so long as the only opposition party was the JSP with an ideological baggage of nationalisation and state control which struck fear in the heart of most business leaders, the LDP would have to be tolerated. Thus, business rallied to the defence of the LDP in the 1990 general election and the LDP held its majority and control of the government. A survey of the business connections of the LDP MPs elected in 1990 also illustrates the complexity of the relationship, and is a good starting point for understanding the extent to which change had occurred (Taketsu, 1992). However, in analysing such a list, it is useful, once again, to distinguish between *seisho*, *seisaku sho* and respectable business leaders.

The two most frequently mentioned business links with LDP politicians were Takeshi Ishihara, President of Nissan, and Yoshiaki Tsutsumi, President of Seibu Railroad. Tsutsumi had been one of the individuals who had personally provided substantial assistance to a range of politicians, including free office space to Takeo Fukuda in the Akasaka Prince Hotel owned by the rail group and loans to a leading member of the Tanaka faction, Ganri Yamashita. In doing so, he gave valuable access to information and the policy-making process in aid of his business (Okamura et al., 1994: 46). This is clearly *seisho*. A number of pharmaceutical firm presidents are also mentioned, and given the importance of government health policy (national health insurance, licensing) for the industry, these might be usefully considered *seisaku sho* as there seems to be a diffuse policy interest at stake rather than the interests of a particular firm.

Business and political change

The situation with Nissan President, Ishihara, is more complex. As noted above, Ishihara was one of the automobile executives who criticised the Takeshita government. Moreover, other export-oriented firms were growing impatient with the type of domestic protectionism represented by the LDP. This included the automobile manufacturer Toyota and the consumer electronics industry, both of which are well represented in the survey. However, a closer look at the reason for their presence is that the business people from these firms held top posts in business organisations. Ishihara was the President of the Keizai Doyukai, an organisation representing top company managers, and Toyota was a vice-president in Keidanren. Ishihara was more outspoken because the independence and progressive history of the Keizai Doyukai permitted him to be so. His connections with politicians, like the connections of the bulk of the business leaders in the survey, seemed to be more a function of his role as a representative of the business community rather than purely firm based or with sectoral interests. Therefore, it was particularly significant when Ishihara and other segments of the organised business community began to move away from the LDP after 1990.

One early if quixotic business-community related attempt to dislodge the LDP was made by the management consultant Omae Kenichi, president of McKinsey & Co. Japan, a subsidiary of the famous US management consulting firm. Omae was author of several best-selling books on business, Japanese competitiveness and government regulation. His best-seller at the time was a book entitled *Heisei Ishin* (Heisei Restoration) which was a detailed programme of critique of existing political practice and proposals for reform. On 25 November, he announced the formation of his *Heisei Ishin no Kai* (Reform of Heisei) which proposed the creation of a federal system in Japan, a shift in foreign policy focus from the US to Asia, an aggressive programme of liberalisation and deregulation based on the market principle, and constitutional revision for recognition of the right of self-defence. While the initial response from his readership was enthusiastic – with over 50,000 members paying 10,000 yen each – but he was unable to attract any national politicians to his cause and was forced to spend a small personal fortune to finance his party despite his membership support. Before long, Omae's voice was lost in the larger changes occurring in Japanese politics, and his supporters drifted away.

The more significant movement from a business point of view

was the *Seiji Kaikaku Suishin Kyogikai* (Political Reform Promotion Association), also known as the *Minkan Seiji Rincho* (Private Political Ethics Commission). The impetus for the formation of the group was the failure of early political reform legislation in the autumn of 1991, though the group was not formally inaugurated until April 1992. The chair of the group was Masao Kamei, special adviser to Nikkeiren, the Japanese Employers Association and a consultant to Sumitomo Electronics, but the group encompassed a number of leading figures from the labour movement, including Chair of the Japanese Trade Union Congress (Rengo), Akira Yamagishi, and academia, such as Uchida Kenzo, as well as other business leaders, such as the new chair of Keidanren, Gaishi Hiraiwa. Most of Japan's top union leaders were members of the group in a personal capacity, including the Public Employees Association, one of the main unions backing the JSP. More important, over 100 MPs from the major political parties had joined the group in a cross-party movement in favour of political reform. Business involvement in these activities clearly indicated it was moving away from the LDP leadership.

The key turning point came in 1992 as a result of the Sagawa and other scandals. At first, the LDP and the other parties in the parliament moved quickly to respond to the scandals by making changes in the Public Election and Political Funds Control Laws on 10 December, including provisions for increased fines for violations of the law, in response to public outrage to the leniency shown to LDP leader Kanemaru arrested as a result of the Sagawa scandal. However, the business community lacked confidence in the ability of the LDP to carry out meaningful reform, and finally turned on the LDP. By April 1993, business leaders supported the *Seiji Kaikaku Suishin Kyogikai* when it published its plans for electoral reform, based on a mixed system of single-member constituencies and proportional representation. The LDP, fearing it would lose seats, refused to accept the proposal.

Rapidly, the business relationship with the LDP deteriorated. Why? Business confidence certainly had grown as major Japanese firms dominated key sectors worldwide, including the automobile and consumer electronics industries. However, this export success was threatened by US threats of retaliation if the Japanese market were not opened to Western goods. Big business, in particular, felt the pressure to deal with deeply submerged interest conflicts between exporters and protected domestic sectors such as agriculture and retailing. In addition, business saw the need to enhance Japan's competitiveness as the country struggled to shake off the recession begun in the aftermath of the Gulf War.

Yet, the main factor was the rise of viable alternatives to the LDP. Business executives made no secret of their desire for a two-party system along US lines with two relatively pro-business parties. Alternation of parties in power promised to make it easier to achieve economic reform and cut the cost of politics for business as they lessened their dependence on the LDP. Auto company executives were most vigorous in their advocacy of change because their firms, employees and labour unions all had interests in direct conflict with core LDP constituencies, but until 1992 the only alternatives – the JSP or the Democratic Socialist Party – were either too far to the left or too small to be viable. By 1992, the Socialist Party began to wane as a threat to the LDP and was moving to moderate its policies in any case. At the same time, new political parties – such as the Japan New Party – emerged as moderate conservative alternatives to the LDP. The Recruit and Sagawa scandals were merely the catalyst for the business community to make a move to reduce its dependence on the LDP.

Business and the fall of the LDP

The first consequence of this change was that the LDP split over the issue of political reform and the mainstream of the business community, led primarily by major export firm business leaders, finally found the courage to distance itself from their long-time ally. The key turning point in the LDP–business relationship came when the leaders of the Keidanren and Keizai Doyukai business organisations indicated that they felt there was a need to rethink political contributions to the LDP which was reeling from the defection of large number of LDP MPs just prior to the 1993 general election. The business community was anticipating a new conservative or centrist group which would enable it to end its dependence on the LDP.

Even the construction industry, which had depended for so many years on profits from public work projects supplied by LDP politicians to their constituencies, was constrained from assisting the party. The search of Kanemaru's home after his arrest on charges related to the Sagawa scandal provided detailed evidence of kickbacks from constructions firms for public works as an unrelated bonus. Under a cloud of scandal, the *Zenekon* (General Federation of

Construction Companies) members ended up giving a limited number of incumbents in the LDP and the LDP breakaway Japan Renewal Party approximately 2 million yen, or one-tenth of what most had requested, and much less than in previous elections. The construction industry had reason to be cautious. On 29 June, the Tokyo Prosecutor's Office arrested the mayor of Sendai and six top managers of four major construction companies for bribery. Since most major firms could also be implicated, the industry and its relations with the LDP were in turmoil. This shift in business support was one of the main factors for the fall of the LDP from power in 1993.

Removal from power was a serious blow to the LDP which in essence was a party of government which managed policy and divided the spoils of office among its supporters. Without access to power and patronage, the party experienced a crisis of confidence. For example, on 24 August 1994, the LDP held a meeting with industrial leaders to discuss the growing strength of the yen which was hurting exports, and the sudden humility of the LDP surprised the participants. The LDP Political Affairs Research Council chair, Ryutaro Hashimoto, began his remarks to the group with the fear that 'Now we have become an opposition party, the greatest concern we had was whether or not you would come or not' (Asahi Shimbun Political Bureau, 1994: 37).

These concerns were to a degree justified as on 2 September, the largest Japanese business association, Keidanren, announced that it would no longer act as a conduit for campaign contributions to political parties from its member corporations. In the past, the many industry associations and interest groups had always thought it useful to have MPs from the LDP as their chairs or in some other symbolic capacity, but given their opposition status, these links also came under question.

While the leadership of the party tried to maintain good relations with business and other interest groups, the party began to fissure and fragment from within. The most pronounced effect of the loss of power was the weakening of LDP factions and rumours of defections from the party to the government coalition. Most LDP members belonged to a faction because they provided the financial support necessary to get elected and gain access to the posts in the party and government necessary to career advancement. Once out of power, LDP access to government posts ended. Moreover, declining business contributions and the prospect of tight political financing legislation

Business and political change

meant severe cutbacks on the amount of funds available to faction members. Some factions even began to consider charging MPs a membership fee. While most MPs maintained their loyalty to the faction which had helped them in the past, those with a loose commitment began to drift away from, or even quit, their faction and, in general, factions seemed less important. The longer the LDP was out of power, the more factions could weaken.

One other change while the LDP was out of power was the passage of political reform legislation. The coalition government which replaced the LDP had committed itself to political reform but there were severe divisions over the issue in the coalition parties. Eventually a compromise deal with the LDP was adopted in January 1994. The main feature of the reform was a new electoral system, but important changes were also made to the system of political funding. Corporate contributions were to be limited to one political group per politician, and corporate contributions limited to 500,000 yen per company per year. By the year 2000, contributions to individuals would be ended and all funds would have to be channelled through political parties. These changes all threatened the LDP way of doing business.

Business returns to the LDP

When the anti-LDP coalition fell in mid-1994, however, the business community began to reverse its earlier distancing from the LDP. It was obvious that the longer the LDP was in power and the longer it took for the anti-LDP opposition to return to office, the more business became wary of alienating the LDP. In late 1995, the Keidanren business federation began to indicate that it would again acts as a conduit for funds to the LDP, but this was just to complete payments already promised. Instead, Keidanren began to encourage more individual business donations and individual business associations affiliated with Keidanren resumed contributions, even though the amounts involved were much less than in the past.

Certain assurances were given by Keidanren, such as the refusal to give money to faction leaders and insistence that they would make donations only to the party itself, but the bulk of the Keidanren funding had been given that way in the past anyway. In addition, it was likely that the magnitude of the contributions would be less than in the past. However, the size and influence of the major firms and business associations assured that the LDP would be well funded while its opponents would have to eke out an existence with public funding and their own meagre resources.

Business was also swayed in its decision to more firmly to back the LDP by the deepening economic crisis in Japan which first manifested itself in the bail-out of the seven Housing Loan Corporations or *Jusen*. The *Jusen* were originally set up to provide reasonable mortgages in order for average Japanese to become homeowners, but during the bubble period, the corporations increasingly lent money for major development projects, including resort facilities and golf courses. The *Jusen* received their funds from a variety of sources, including the major Japanese banks, but a large proportion of their finance was supplied through the Agricultural Cooperative Banks. The Agricultural Cooperative Banks were also awash with money in the late 1980s and early 1990s and invested heavily in *Jusen*, which were considered a relatively safe investment. Though the figure continued to grow, by mid-1995, the *Jusen* held over 7 trillion yen in bad debt and were unable to pay their creditors, including the Agricultural Cooperative Banks which were in financial difficulties themselves for similar reasons. Given that the LDP was heavily involved at the local level in the agricultural cooperatives, they needed to act. Therefore the government proposed a reorganisation plan for the *Jusen* which involved the injection of 685 billion yen of public monies as part of the restructuring. This meant that every man, woman and child in Japan was be forced to pay 5,500 yen in additional taxes to save these financial institutions.

The opposition demanded full disclosure of Finance Ministry information on the scale of the crisis, and publication of the information created an uproar as the situation was far worse than the government had led the public to believe. A number of large loans had inadequate collateral to back them and some involved questionable deals between financial institutions and individuals associated with organised crime. However, the main goal of the business community was Japanese financial stability and the murky issue of the pursuit of responsibility for the crisis could not be allowed to endanger that goal. Business once again fully backed the LDP.

Thus, a shift of business away from the LDP had helped to remove the party from power in 1993, and once out of power, business was able to operate more freely. Once the LDP returned to power, however, they had to be placated by the business community and the old relationship was resumed. Moreover, the growing economic crisis

Business and political change

led business to support LDP efforts to bail-out stricken financial institutions. The LDP's interests and those of business were so deeply tied with the troubled financial institutions that the rethink of the relationship between business and politicians was shelved indefinitely. In fact, the major banks – once key contributors to the LDP – have now become dependent on a government bail-out for their survival.

Business still has an agenda but it is no longer clear that the LDP has the will to pursue it. Industry has been eager to pursue deregulation of the economy as a first step to reinvigorating the Japanese economy. In particular, they hope to emulate US success in producing sustained economic growth through reductions in transportation and communication costs. However, the regulations business seeks to change protect LDP clients in the trucking industry and the telecommunications industry. The LDP has made general promises to cut bureaucracy and has proposed a radical reorganisation of the bureaucracy with a reduction in the number of public employees, but the timetable for change in the key areas sought by business leaders reflects LDP reluctance to confront difficult trade-offs. As a result, progress in reform has been glacial.

Business dissatisfaction was most obvious during the re-election of the former Prime Minister, Obuchi, as LDP president in the summer of 1998. An old right-wing soldier, Seiroku Kajiyama, was championed by business as their best hope for reform but did not win because leadership selection in the LDP is determined by deals between factions and Kajiyama had only one major faction behind him. Indeed, the failure of the Kajiyama candidacy demonstrates the limits of business influence and business understanding of political dynamics. There was little evidence that Kajiyama would have made much of a difference except he had ties to Ichiro Ozawa and his Liberals. Ozawa has been a consistent voice in favour of radical reform even before he split from the LDP in 1993 and helped bring the party temporarily out of government. However, even when the Liberals did eventually join in a surprise coalition with the LDP in 1999, it would be hard to argue that the results in terms of economic reforms have been impressive. Business dissatifaction continues.

Conclusion: the private and public of political business

This chapter is not the place to untangle the cross-cutting cleavages and overlapping interests under the surface in Japan today. The aim of this chapter was merely to demonstrate the limits of business influence over political change. Responsible business tends to feel it has the right to criticise the LDP even if there are limits to the political power of business to control the party, especially when it is in power and business needs the LDP to create a policy environment condusive to its interests. This leads to a need to understand the policy context in which all business is enmeshed and the organisational context which establishes and limits the political 'right to speak' for responsible business, both of which are addressed in later chapters.

At the same time, it could also be argued that business interests continue to play a major role in the formulation of Japanese public policy precisely because some businesses are successfully resisting reform while others have forced the issue of reform on to the political agenda. Therefore, all areas of deregulation being sought have continuing political implications. For example, financial services deregulation involves the survival of existing struggling firms, successful firms seeking new business and opportunities for expansion, foreign firms eager to exploit their experience with deregulated markets, and powerful governmental agencies such as the post office with powerful political patrons. Similarly, communication deregulation involves the former NTT monopoly against its new competitors, and transportation costs impinge on the long-standing LDP clients in the Truckers Association. Finally, there is a serious debate about the extensive use of public works to boost the sluggish economy – to the benefit of constructions companies – rather than tax cuts – which might benefit consumer goods manufacturers or financial institutions. The dynamics of these policy trade-offs will be discussed in Part II.

First, however, a background to the role of money is needed to understand the relationship between business and politics. Money is the essential glue that binds together the relationship between firms, industries and politicians. Thus, the issues raised by corporate money in politics will be examined in some detail in the next chapter.

4

The regulation of business money in politics

In the previous chapters we have examined the historical trends of the relationship between business and politicians in Japan. There has been an implicit assumption that there is a necessary bond between the articulation of business interests and the activities of politicians acting on behalf of business. This chapter confronts the concrete manifestation of this relationship: the supply of political funds from firms to politicians and political parties.

We begin with an examination of the historical and institutional framework regulating political finance, including important changes at several key junctures. This is needed to examine the reasons for change and assess their impact. This historical discussion leads directly to the issue of prohibition of business funding to individual politicians. These cases reveal the range of possible outcomes in the regulation or prohibition of forms of political finance, including a number of loopholes. The chapter concludes with a discussion of recent revelations of questionable political fundraising which demonstrates the limits of change.

Historical background

It is always difficult to know when to start a discussion of the historical background to political finance and related issues of corruption in Japan. Corruption certainly existed in the Tokugawa period (1600–1868) before the opening of Japan to the West. If the numerous period dramas on Japanese television or in films and other media are to be believed, then the problem was endemic. In fact, however, these images of scandal in feudal Japan are a not very subtle commentary on the issue of corruption in contemporary Japan. These are based on modern images rather than well-researched historical cases. Moreover, it is doubtful that the Japanese legacy is much worse than that of Jacksonian democracy in the US or British 'rotten boroughs'.

It is also unnecessary to document the scandals of prewar Japan (i.e. before Japan's defeat in 1945) which occurred under an autocratic regime with weak democratic elements. Of course, one of the weaknesses of prewar Japanese party democracy was the persistent allegation of corruption. The two major parties were bankrolled extensively by the two largest economic conglomerates (*zaibatsu*) – Mitsui and Mitsubishi – and the main focus of politicians was to bring concrete benefits to their constituents. Indeed, the party in power usually won the election by using government largesse to secure the vote so that it was only autocratic interference which made alternation of parties in power possible.

With the advent of universal male suffrage in the general election of 1928, the cost of securing the vote escalated. Politics became more of an economic risk to those involved even if it required only small gifts (sake, dried fish, etc.) to reinforce the loyalties of poor tenant farmers. This prewar legacy of gifts at election time should not be confused with the gift-giving 'tradition' of postwar Japan. Like Christmas in the West, especially in the US, the twice yearly gift-giving of *oseibo* and *chugen* have been commercialised to such a degree that it is easy to forget the elite origins of the practice. It is only in the postwar period that large numbers of Japanese joined the ambitious postwar middle class and adopted the practice of annual ritual gift-giving to secure status and advancement for themselves or their children. In any case, the parallel is inexact as election gifts reverse the traditional tendency for social gifts to go from the lower to the higher status.

Therefore, it was ironically the democratisation of Japan which made politics more expensive and corruption more widespread as elites felt increasingly compelled to reach out to voters. The 'levelling' effect of the war and the democratisation reforms of the Allied Occupation of Japan (1945–52) after the war merely reinforced this tendency. Parties were given a key position in the new political order. Universal suffrage created large numbers of new voters with the addition of women voters. Land reform meant that tenants became independent farmers, and the landlords who were at the centre of the prewar parties effectively disappeared as an important political force.

In this context, parties were desperate for funds with the collapse of the traditional financial backers and needed new sources of

Regulation of business money in politics

support. The end of the war also created a new type of entrepreneur in the form of black market traders. These underground sources of funding were important to the fledgling political parties of immediate postwar Japan (Wildes, 1948). Not surprisingly, the Japanese governments of the day were soon rocked by scandal, the coal nationalisation and Showa Denko scandals. The coal nationalisation scandal arose in 1947 when the JSP, then the leader of a coalition government, put forward legislation for the nationalisation of the coal industry. The Socialists' coalition partner, the Democratic Party, was officially committed to assisting the passage of the legislation as well, but a large number of Democratic MPs remained opposed to the legislation and voted against it. A few of these opponents were later accused of accepting bribes from industry representatives to ensure the defeat of the legislation and, although three were convicted, two were found innocent on appeal. The Showa Denko scandal also involved a major industry which was part of the Socialist–Democratic economic plan for subsidising core industries – including coal, steel and fertilisers. Showa Denko produced fertiliser and several politicians, including the sitting Prime Minister, Hitoshi Ashida, were accused of accepting bribes in exchange for the subsidies in 1948. While Ashida and four other politicians were cleared of the charges, two others were found guilty but given suspended sentences.

As a result of these scandals, a Political Funds Control Law was passed in July 1948. It required parties to report the amounts of political contributions received, and placed severe restrictions on campaign activities, including the amount spent. Most of the restrictions governed the behaviour of candidates in the official campaign period just prior to the election. Only limited numbers of posters were allowed at specified locations, and door-to-door canvassing was prohibited. While these restrictions were aimed at prewar abuses, such as wealthier candidates' use of extensive printed posters or attempts at voter intimidation by prewar landlords or other local notables, postwar economic and land reforms made these restrictions seem outdated. Nonetheless, they are still in effect today and have been extended to restrictions on the use of television advertising and even Internet websites.

The Socialist–Democratic coalition collapsed as a result of the Showa Denko scandal, and the Liberal Party gained power. When the Socialists regained their strength in the mid-1950s, the business community encouraged the Liberal and the Democratic Parties to merge, and the conservative LDP has been the dominant party in Japan ever since. Moreover, the continuing threat of Socialist gains with continued urbanisation in the late 1950s compelled Keidanren to act as a conduit for political donations to the LDP. The LDP formed a political funds control organisation, *Kokumin Seiji Kyokai* (People's Political Association), in 1961 and Keidanren helped to orchestrate business contributions to the fund. Since Keidanren is a federation of business organisations, each organisation was expected to provide a share of funds based on the economic strength of its constituent members. The money raised was provided from the firms directly to the LDP. In addition, individual industry associations and firms continued to supply an even greater amount to individual politicians and, in particular, to faction leaders such as Kishi, Ikeda and Sato, who were potential (if not actual) Prime Ministers (Iyasu, 1984: 107). With generous funding, the LDP could stave off the threat from the left, and individual industries and firms could also try to influence politicians to support their interests at the same time.

The invulnerability of LDP politicians

It is not just preferential access to funds which placed the LDP in a better position than their rivals; the MPs of the party were also relatively invulnerable to prosecution if they violated the political funding laws. Indeed, candidates almost invariably spent above the amounts stipulated by law. In fact, Prime Minister Yoshida – the leader of Japan for most of the ten years after the Second World War – is quoted in 1954 as saying 'party government would come to an end if it abided by the Political Funds Control Law' (Yanaga, 1968: 130). Politicians were able to avoid prosecution for these violations by rigorously claiming only the legal amount in their reports. When they were caught over-spending they were often able to successfully shift blame to their political agents, campaign workers and even family members. Those who were prosecuted and convicted were rarely given prison sentences and most were found innocent on appeal.

Another problem has been that the control of the system to prosecute politicians is itself not immune from political interference. A clear example of this problem was the case of the former Prime Minister, Eisaku Sato, at the time that he was only a Liberal Party cabinet minister. Sato was implicated in a shipbuilding scandal in the mid-1950s and was only saved from prosecution by the intervention

Regulation of business money in politics

of the Liberal Party Home Ministry who blocked his arrest and indictment despite public outrage. Sato continued to be elected to parliament and eventually became one of the longest serving postwar Prime Ministers (1964–72) and, so, allegations of corruption never ultimately harmed his career.

The legality of contributions has also been challenged in the courts to no effect. In April 1961, a stockholder in Hachiman Steel sued the president and a member of the board of directors of the company for using corporate funds to make a political donation to the LDP. He argued that the company's articles of incorporation indicated that the purpose of the firm was to produce and sell steel so the diversion of funds to political purposes was an illegal violation of the articles of incorporation (Kobayashi, 1976: 51). While the first trial ended in victory for the stockholder, in 1970 the Japanese Supreme Court reversed the lower court decision and upheld the right of corporations to make political donations as they too were legal entities entitled to the same rights as individual citizens. This decision was not surprising given that the LDP has maintained control over the appointment of judges for many years.

In addition, prosecutors became reluctant to pursue allegations of corruption because politicians were able to interfere with the prosecution itself. For example, there were no major scandals in Japan between 1968 and the Lockheed scandal in 1976 because it is alleged that the prosecutor feared the reaction of politicians after one prosecutor's career was damaged by politicians implicated in the Kyowa Sugar incident of 1968. At least forty-eight politicians were investigated and though only one indictment (against MP Fumio Abe) resulted, the lesson of taking on politicians was not lost on other prosecutors (Uozumi, 1997: 68–7). Indeed, the LDP also has control over the prosecutors' office as it does over the careers of judges so there is little incentive for the legal establishment to challenge individual LDP politicians.

The exception came in 1976 as a result of the Lockheed scandal. Former Prime Minister Tanaka was tried and convicted on bribery charges as a result of the scandal but only after the allegations had been made public by a US Senate investigation into corruption. Tanaka was also unfortunate that his successor as Prime Minister, Takeo Miki, had a reputation for opposing corruption and allowed the charges to be brought. Nonetheless, Tanaka never served any time in prison as a result of his conviction because he used his continuing influence to make sure his faction controlled the Ministry of Justice and delayed the proceeding for as long as possible. As a result, he remained out of prison during the lengthy appeals process. Overall, LDP MPs have been relatively invulnerable to punishment even if caught and this fact encourages them to create dubious links with a variety of firms. This is not an isolated case.

Attempts to strengthen the law after 1975

In the aftermath of Tanaka's fall and the Lockheed scandal, new laws were introduced in 1975 to require stricter limits on and reporting of campaign contributions. Contributions were determined by the level of a corporation's capitalisation, with a annual maximum of 100 million yen for the largest corporations. Corporations could donate no more than 1.5 million per year to any one individual or political group. However, the gaping loophole in the law was that individual politicians were permitted to set up an unlimited number of political groups to collect such donations.

The problem was that the competition for factions continued to be intense and their need for funds continued unabated. Tanaka continued to exercise influence behind the scenes and even cut short Fukuda's brief stint in power by funding the purchase of party memberships to deny Fukuda a second term as party president and Prime Minister. In fact, the uncertainty of factional politics led the business community to feel compelled to fund all sides to be safe (Daimondo Sha, 1980: 205).

While the old establishment firms, such as those in the steel industry and banking sector, declined temporarily, the loss was more than covered by the rise of construction firms and other new business interests. The Recruit scandal (1988–89) was a clear example of new firms eager to contribute. Hiromasa Ezoe, the president of Recruit, knew that he could not depend on only one faction or individual to maintain an influence so he gave money to all and sundry. As a result nearly all LDP factions were implicated in the scandal (the exception being the faction of Toshio Komoto, the successor to Takeo Miki) and the inability of the faction leaders to become Prime Minister led to the selection of the relatively unknown Toshiki Kaifu in 1989 from the untainted Komoto faction. It should be remembered that the Miki/Komoto faction is also the weakest in number of MPs.

One change initiated as a result of the Recruit scandal was the

Regulation of business money in politics

passage of insider trading laws which had been surprisingly lax in Japan. Indeed, it was only in April 1989 that Japan had a law prohibiting insider trading. Until that point, politicians would often receive such information and even unlisted shares as an indirect form of political contribution to get around the legal restrictions on the amount donated. Moreover, many politicians were among the small number of favoured clients who were compensated by major brokerage firms when the value of their shares fell after the bubble began to collapse in the early 1990s. This, too, was finally made illegal in January 1992.

Even so, the relationship between politicians and stock market investments continued to be problematic. In 1998, an LDP MP, Shokei Arai, was stripped of his parliamentary immunity as a result of allegations that he received illegal 'top-up' profits as a result of his share dealings with Nissho Securities. These transactions came to light as Nomura Securities and Nissho Securities were being investigated for providing similar services to a *sokaiya* organised crime figure. Arai never came to trial due to his suicide on the day of losing his immunity from prosecution. However, it did temporarily raise public interest in the issue and brokerage firms admitted that politicians still received favourable treatment, including preferential allocations of equities about to go public for which there is heavy demand (*Asahi Shimbun*, 19 February 1998). Therefore, it is not difficult to believe the tabloid magazine in Japan which reported in 1999 that one of their reporters had been threatened by a senior faction leader in the LDP over an article exposing the fact that the MP concerned had received a tip-off about the collapse of a major bank and was able to sell his shares before the failure was made public (*Shukan Hoseki*, 29 July 1999).

Thus, even though the laws relating to the use of insider information and share compensation have been strengthened, there is still considerable ambiguity over the use of corporate assets for political purposes. The use of employees in support of candidates, noted in an earlier discussion of the 1974 Upper House election, continues. The resignation of the chair of the Chamber of Commerce and Industry in 1994 was in part due to the revelation that his firm, Kajima construction, had sent employees to help in election campaigns. Similarly, the use of construction company officials has been noted in the case of Ozawa's campaign in the 1995 Upper House election.

Indeed, Upper House elections are particularly likely to see industry-supported campaigns due to a segment of the Upper House being elected by proportional representation on a national basis so rewarding industry-wide action. This phenomenon was noted in the 1998 Upper House election as well, with a former Tokyo Electric Power candidate supported not only by the industry, but also by the Electric Power Workers General Federation, which has always been close to the industry but has grown even closer with the demise of the left. Indeed, apologists of industry-supported candidates point to the legitimacy of union supported candidates and argue the same tolerance should be shown to industry-led campaigns.

Questions are raised, however, when firms use their assets in ways which might seem to be a method of avoiding the strictures of the Political Funds Control Act and related laws. For example, should the labour costs of employees active on campaigns be counted as a corporate contribution? This issue was raised in the early 1990s when Tokyo Electric Power, which had announced that it would not make political contributions due to its status as a public utility, nonetheless was discovered in 1993 to be paying a generous rate for advertising space in the LDP newsletter in what appeared to be a hidden donation (Kubota, 1997: 129). Is the purchase of services or goods from a party a donation to that party? Similarly, Yoshiro Nakajima, an LDP MP arrested for falsifying expenditure reports to illegally receive public subsidies, had also been using free office space and clerical support provided by Fuji Heavy Industries between 1994 and the time of his arrest in 1998. The LDP was in trouble for failing to mention the donation, but the firm denied knowledge of who used the facilities.

Further attempts at reform in 1994

The Political Funds Control Law was strengthened once again in the aftermath of the Sagawa scandal in 1992. These changes were largely made possible by the fall of the LDP from power and the formation of an anti-LDP coalition government committed to political reform. There was an initial problem, however, in that the JSP – a key member of the coalition – also stood to lose from some of the reforms (primarily a new election system), so many renegade JSP MPs joined with the LDP in blocking the reforms. As a result, the LDP in opposition was still able to water down or delay changes.

Political donations were one area in which the LDP ability to delay reform served them well. The aim of the original reform plan was to strengthen political parties by prohibiting corporate donations to individual MPs, so all funds would have to be disbursed through the party. The LDP had the implemenation of this prohibition delayed until the end of 1999. They did accept, however, that individual MPs could only received donations directly from individuals, companies and political groups through a single registered fund. Individuals are permitted to contribute 1.5 million yen per year whereas companies and political groups are limited to 500,000 yen so long as they are permitted to continue. Political parties, on the other hand, can receive up to 20 million yen from individuals, and between 7.5 to 100 million from companies and political groups, depending on the size of the firm or group.

In addition, parties were provided with a public subsidy from a fund based on the amount of 250 yen per person to be distributed among the parties based on their share of the vote. In a bid to encourage larger and stronger parties, the larger party received subsidies greater that a simple proportion of their size, and parties with less than 2 per cent of the vote receive nothing. However, the public money would not constitute more than two-thirds of the previous year's income of the party, exclusive of public funds and loans. These public monies were intended to wean parties from their dependency on corporate contributions.

Almost immediately after the legislation was passed, however, the parliamentary secretaries of MPs began to explore the new laws and found considerable loopholes. The status of income from the sale of publications and tickets for political receptions was unclear under the new law. Both were major sources of income, and the announcement by one party, the Harbinger Party, that it would begin to sell tickets to its own receptions – despite a high-profile pledge not to do so – underscored the importance of this source of income (*Yomiuri Shimbun*, 25 September 1994). It was also unclear if the contributions by individual corporate officers would be counted as a prohibited corporate donation or not, since the possibility of corporate donations channelled through individuals would appear to undermine the new law.

This last loophole of individual contributions did not become a problem, however, as individual donations fell well short of substituting for corporate funding. As a result, the LDP continued to debate the weakening of funding rules to permit business to continue to directly contribute to individual MPs right up to the 31 December 1999 deadline for prohibition. At first, the LDP announced their intention of ignoring the deadline and continuing with corporate donations as usual. However, under pressure from their coalition partners, the

Figure 4.1 Political contributions in Japan (1978–99)

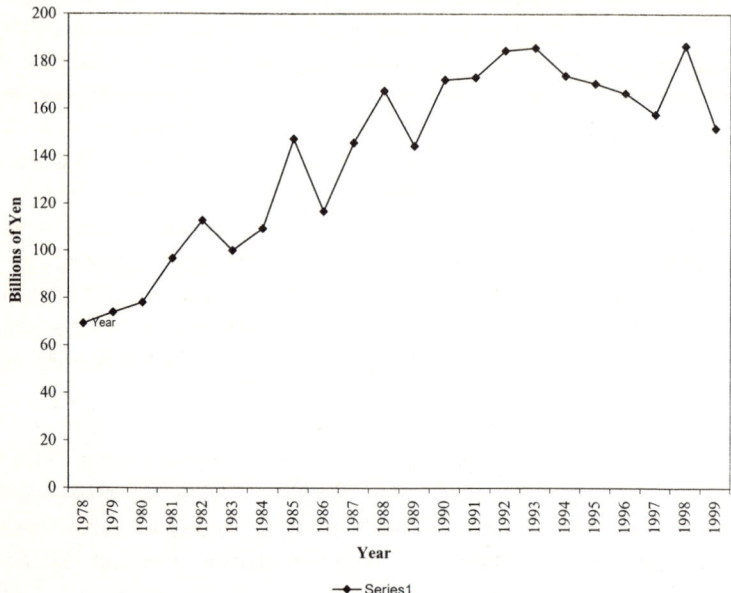

Source: Ministry of Home Affairs, *Heisei 11 Nenbun Seiji Shikin Shushi Hokoku no Gaiyo* (Summary of the Report on Political Funds Income for the Year 2000).

Komeito and Liberal Party, the LDP reluctantly agreed to prohibit corporate donations to individuals. The problem was that the LDP's solution raised more questions than it answered. Corporate donations to the local branches of the LDP were still permitted, but since the local branches are invariably controlled by the local MP, the branch became simply a new channel for corporate contributions to individuals MPs.

It should be noted, however, the amount of money being donated to political parties has been in decline in any case. The Ministry of Home Affairs annual reports on political spending reveal that political contributions had fallen every year since 1993, with the exception of 1998 (Figure 4.1). The main cause was the decline in corporate contributions to the LDP. Some businesses took the opportunity at the time of the demise of the LDP as a party of government to reduce their contributions overall. Others, unsure of how long any of the coalitions was going to last, thought the safest course was to give a little money to each of the major parties so as not to offend any. Contributions to factions and individual politicians were hardest hit,

Regulation of business money in politics

and major politicians inside and outside the LDP increasingly relied on bank loans to finance their political careers.

To a large degree, this decline in corporate contributions can be explained by the end of Keidanren's role as a conduit for political funds for the LDP announced in 1993. It seemed as if the organisation might resume contributions after the LDP returned to office in 1994 when it announced that it would continue to organise and help deliver the contributions promised to the ruling party prior to 1993. However, the Keidanran official with whom I spoke in July 1999 emphatically denied that the organisation played any role in organising political contributions, though it has tried to promote individual political donations by corporate executives, through the *Kigyojin Seiji Foramu* [Entrepreneur Political Forum] created by it in July 1996. This has been noticeably unsuccessful.

The unchanging role of money politics

In the mean time, the most recent figures for political contributions show the continuing presence of business funding, especially for the LDP. For example, in the summer of 1999, the Japan Construction Industry Association Federation organised the raising of 370 million yen in contributions to LDP MPs in what appeared to many to be a payback for generous spending on public works approved by the party, but this was not revealed until the end of the year (*Nikkan Gendai*, 28 December 1999).

Moreover, it is not just the LDP. Nearly all the political parties continue to be highly dependent on corporate funds. Indeed, the more viable the party, the more likely they are to be given corporate contributions as Table 4.1 makes clear. The LDP is most dependent on business contributions, followed closely by their coalition partners, the Komeito and Liberal Party. The main opposition party, the Democratic Party is more evenly balance between sources. The Social Democratic Party is the most successful in gathering individual donations, but the party is small and weak, and the amounts involved are negligible in comparison with those of the LDP and the Democratic Party. It must be remember that these are donations to both parties and individuals.

In 1998 when the bail-out of financial institutions by LDP-led governments made it politically unpopular to receive bank contributions, the banks announced their intention to stop funding the LDP. Even then, the banks continued to provide funds until debts were

Table 4.1 Political donations to MPs by party and source, 1998 (in percentages)

	Party					
Source	LDP	Democratic	Komeito	Liberal	Social Democratic	Total
Individuals	16.7	41.4	35.1	18.1	94.5	19.7
Firms and groups	83.3	58.5	64.9	81.9	5.5	80.3

Source: *Yomiuri Shimbun*, 10 September 1999.

repaid, and the regional banks still give generously. Moreover, three of the regional banks which were the recipients of public infusions of cash, made political contributions in 1998 despite the major banks and long-term credit banks upholding their pledge to refuse to make political contributions so long as they were using public funds to cover their losses (*Yomiuri Shimbun*, 10 September 1999).

In addition, the list of the top political donors is headed by the usual suspects. The top donor was still the steel industry. The automobile industry continues it tradition of providing funding to the moderate left. Moreover, Ozawa's Liberal Party also benefited from corporate generosity, but these figures reflect 1998 when the party had entered a coalition agreement with the LDP.

Overall, the industries represented have changed little over time. In fact, similar firms top the 1999 list (Table 4.2). This time, however, only three firms donated amounts over 30 million yen: Toyota Automobiles (65.4 million to the LDP and Liberal Party), Nishimatsu Construction (39.9 million to the LDP and Liberal Party), and Japan Steel (30 million to the LDP alone). Sixteen other firms donated between 30 and 20 million yen; in order of amount from highest to lowest are Toshiba, Matsushita Electrical Industries, Suzuki, Suntory, Nissan Automobiles, Toyo Construction, Obayashi Construction, Taisei Construction, Sony, Hitachi, Itosei Trading, Mitsui Trading, Mitsubishi Trading, Denso (auto parts) and Toda Construction (*Nihon Keizai Shimbun*, 7 September 2000).

What is even more surprising is that firms in financial difficulty or implicated in wrongdoing are often found among the list of major political donors. This included the high-profile Sogo which made several contributions to the LDP and three LDP MPs just prior to dis-

Regulation of business money in politics

Table 4.2 Firms and assocations donating 30 million yen or more, 1998 (millions of yen)

	Party		
	LDP	Democratic	Liberal
Associations			
Japan Steel Federation	90.0		70.0
Japan Automobile Industry Association	85.1	9.1	
Japan Electrical Industry Association	70.0		
Tokyo Stock Exchange Members Council	65.8		
Petroleum Federation	60.0		
Cement Council	45.0		
Petrochemical Industries Council	45.0		
Japan Chemical Fibres Council	40.0		
Estate Agents/Real Estate Council	37.5		
National Trust Banks Council	35.0		
Department Stores Council	35.0		
Firms			
Toyota Automobiles	56.3	9.1	
NEC	40.0		
Toda Construction	32.5	1.1	6.6
Nissan Automobiles	30.9	3.3	
Taisei Construction	30.0	2.0	1.2
Japan Steel	30.0		

Source: Yomiuri Shimbun, 10 September 1999.

solution. In addition, three insurance firms which have gone bankrupt also made donations to the LDP and LDP MPs. Just as questionable are two construction firms struggling with debt as a result of the collapse of the bubble economy, which made generous donations to the LDP in 1998 (*Nihon Keizai Shimbun*, 7 September 2000). Finally, the firms involved in a bid-rigging scheme in Hokkaido being pursued by the Japan Fair Trade Commission, donated money to both the LDP, including Prime Minister Mori, and the leader of the opposition Democratic Party, Yukio Hatoyama (*Yomiuri Shimbun*, 8 September 2000).

Thus, the evidence for suspecting that little will change in the dubious nature of the relationship between business and the LDP is compelling. Business has always tended to develop an unseemly close relationship with the LDP as the perpetual party of government. With the lack of alternation of parties in power, as we have seen, these interest group links become fixed with the ruling party. At the same time, these links are continuously being renewed. For example, the factional leadership of the LDP has just been renewed with the influx of dynamic new leaders. Moreover, the new stricter rules governing political fundraising and the provision of public financing for political parties have not stopped allegations of serious impropriety.

It is not surprising then that all of the new major faction leaders have been implicated in past political contribution scandals. For example, in January 1996 it was alleged by the leader of his local constituency organisation that the then LDP Party Secretary, Koichi Kato, had received 1 million yen as illegal campaign contributions from a failed leisure complex developer who had been convicted of bribing public officials. This did not stop Kato from becoming the new leader of the Miyazawa faction in early 1999 and actively campaigning to become prime minister in late 1999 and early 2000.

Similarly, Taku Yamazaki took control of the bulk of the old Nakasone faction in early 1999 despite his implication in scandal. The scandal involved a petroleum wholesaler which received a total of 640 million yen over the period from 1992 to 1994 from Mitsubishi Petroleum and Mitsui Mining to act as their agent. Mitsui Mining also provided the wholesaler with an unrecovered 240 million yen short-term loan. None of these amounts were declared for tax purposes. The connection to Yamazaki was that the wholesaler admitted giving 20 million yen to Yamazaki as a political contribution. While Yamazaki did nothing wrong himself, the reliance of politicians on suspect funds raises the issue of how aware and responsible politicians should be for the sources of their funds. Despite these questions, Yamazaki has become a major LDP faction leader and has indicated his interest in becoming Prime Minister as well.

Finally, there is the case of Yoshiro Mori who assumed control of the Hiroshi Mitsuzuka (former Abe) faction in early 1999. He was one of the MPs involved in the Recruit scandal of 1988–89 in which he obtained a 10 million yen profit when the Recruit shares he received were subsequently listed on the Tokyo stock exchange. His name was also mentioned in connection with the Sagawa Express scandal of

Regulation of business money in politics

1992, in which he has strongly denied any involvement. Finally, when the president of a petroleum wholesaler, Junichi Izumii was arrested on tax evasion charges, he claimed to have given Mori 10 million yen in contributions but Mori only admits to have dinner with Izumii three times. Mori has played a balancing role between the faction of the former Prime Minister Obuchi, and the ambitious Kato and Yamazaki factions. When Obuchi was forced to resign due to illness in early 2000, Mori became Prime Minister.

In the early days of the Mori administration, the construction industry relationship with politicians was once again called into question. This time the faction of Takami Eto and Shizuka Kamei was tainted by scandal when one of the faction's members, Eiichi Nakao, was arrested for receiving a bribe from a construction company to interfere with a competitive tendering process while he was Construction Minister in 1996. The Eto–Kamei faction had wanted to secure the valuable post of Construction Minister again in the Mori government formed in July 2000, but was forced to give up their claim to the post due to the implication of their faction in the scandal. Thus, this faction too was implicated in impropriety.

This means all the top leadership of the LDP continues to be tainted with scandal. The three faction leaders mentioned above – Kato, Yamazaki and Mori – are the key figures who made the Hashimoto (1996–98) and Obuchi (1998–2000) governments possible. In fact, most top LDP leaders have been implicated in dubious fundraising. Given that the overwhelming majority of Japanese Prime Ministers have continued in office for only a few years, then one of these scandal-tainted politicians will become prime minister, perpetuating an image of corruption.

This leaves the question of the faction of the former Prime Minister Obuchi. By the summer of 2000, the former Prime Minister Hashimoto was leader of this faction which can be traced directly back to Takeshita and Tanaka. There is no need to repeat here the serious scandals which have plagued this faction, but one should note that Hashimoto himself was forced to resign as the result of a securities scandal in 1992 while he was Finance Minister, though this did not stop him from becoming Prime Minister in 1996. Thus, even if the former Obuchi faction should regain its strength and influence, the problem of tainted leaders will continue.

Yet, there is one recent sign of possible change. In the aftermath of the revelations of the Construction Minister corruption scandal in the summer of 2000, the opposition parties began to suggest that *assen* be made illegal. This was later adopted by the LDP's coalition partners, the Komeito and, reluctantly, by the LDP itself. *Assen* is where a politician receives a contribution from a firm or group and then intervenes on behalf of that firm or group with the bureaucracy or local authorities. The legislation, which came into effect in February 2001, makes it a crime for an MP or an MP's three publicly funded secretaries to engage in this activity if they have received a donation from the petitioner. However, there are several possible loopholes. First, it is unclear who will be prohibited from acting on behalf of firms and groups if donations are given to the party as a whole or even to local branches. Second, private secretaries are excluded from the law and politicians also use such persons for these activities. Finally, there is a fear that it will drive contributions underground given the need for firms and groups to be assured that they have politicians to make the case for them to government agencies.

The possibility of continuing illegal contributions leads back to the overall problem outlined in this chapter; namely, there is no process by which the LDP can be sanctioned even in the face of widespread public disgust at the use of loopholes or outright violations of the law. That is, even though the general public is strongly opposed to corrupt practices or even the appearance of impropriety, there is no judicial means by which the LDP can be controlled, nor is there a political channel by which the public can make their views heard. Even elections are imperfect vehicles to register protest. The general election in June 2000 was limited in its impact due the nature of the single member constituency system. Japanese voters vote for the individual MP and rely less on party affiliation even compared with US voters and certainly are less party-label oriented than British voters. Given high levels of support in their home districts, the major leaders of the LDP were re-elected by comfortable margins. There was a backlash against the party as a whole in 2000, but it was merely a case of the LDP losing urban seats which it should have lost long ago. The vulnerability of the LDP and problems with money politics in Japan seem set to continue.

Conclusion

This seems to lead to the depressing conclusion that little has changed despite changes in the legal framework governing political finance.

Regulation of business money in politics

However, such an assessment may be too negative for two reasons. The first is that it assumes a basic illegitimacy of political finance by business in the first place. That is, the mere fact of a business political donation to a politician does not automatically mean there is a corrupt relationship. If one accepts the idea that the financing of political activity by business is legitimate, then the issue is not whether or not money reaches politicians but what type of money, to which politicians and under what circumstances. The second reason is that the new rules for the prohibition of contributions to individual politicians has only just begun and it may be that old practices will cease to be an issue. It is too early to determine if the prohibition on funding to individuals and instead the channelling of funds to specific local branches of the party will have a positive impact. A discussion of the possible consequences of the new rules will be reserved for the concluding chapter.

The key point to be made is that political leaders continue to rely on contributions which – even though not always illegal in themselves – sometimes rely on illegally obtained funds in which Japan was awash especially in the period of the bubble economy. Japanese politicians created the bubble through their economic policies and reaped the benefits in various ways, both straightforward and dubious. There is no indication that these practices have ended, and the process of deregulation and continuation of massive public works spending to stimulate the stagnant Japanese economy, not to mention persistent allegations of impropriety, indicate that past practices continue unabated. Worse, the relationship between business and politicians has gone from being simple ties of mutual interest to a structural compulsion to find new ways to create opportunities for gain.

The underlying question considered in this chapter is why have institutional arrangements failed to effectively regulate political finance in Japan? It is certainly not because of inherent corruption in Japanese political culture. It is also not because the rules were too strict. They were simply outdated and not fully enforced. Any laws are enacted based on the assumption that the authorities have the will and the ability to enforce the law. As we have seen, this was institutionally difficult for political reasons. In fact, the institutional basis of policy making even seems to make the situation worse, as the next three chapters demonstrate

Part II

Business and the policy-making process

5

The bureaucratic context of business politics

It is not unusual for those engaged in business to see politics as a nuisance. They view politicians and politically minded bureaucrats as interfering in the smooth operation of the market, or tampering with the key institutional features of the economy under which they operate. However, there is no such thing as an unregulated free market. The choice is between different forms of institutional regulation of markets with variable consequences for specific industries and firms. Changes in institutions and policies sought by one industry or group of firms to 'reduce regulation' may be seen by others as 'interfering in the smooth operations of the market'. Given the complexities of conflicting interests, agreement on the optimal set of institutions and policies is impossible. Politics is a natural process of adjustment between potentially incompatible claims.

This chapter, and the two which follow it, will examine policy making and demonstrate the institutional context in which policy is made. The literature covering this area is massive if one includes the numerous studies which focus on the detail of specific reforms in specific industries. Therefore, this study will avoid controversies over the content of reform. Yet, it will still be able to show how institutional context profoundly shapes the behaviour of businesses, bureaucrats and politicians. In particular, it will outline the obstacles to economic reform and explain how the institutional context in Japan does change despite serious impediments to speedy reform. In fact, it will be shown that the transformation process tends to lead to a reinforcement of structural corruption and collusive practices. This point will be significant for the later discussion of transparency and regulation.

Existing approaches

The general literature on policy making in Japan is relatively manageable. In fact, there are few monographs in Japanese or English focused solely on Japanese policy making. The only one of recent note is Minoru Nakano's *The Policymaking Process in Contemporary Japan* (1997). Studies of specific industries or issues are much more common, for example Robert Uriu's *Troubled Industries* (1996) on declining industries in Japan and Steven Vogel's book (1996) on comparative financial deregulation in Japan, France and the UK. There have been chapters in books on Japanese politics, including textbooks, which have been very influential in shaping perceptions of the policy-making process. This is particular true with Ramseyers and Rosenbluth's *Japan's Political Marketplace* (1993) with its notion of principle–agent theory applied to the relationship between politicians and bureaucrats discussed below. Therefore, there is more than enough material on which to base a general discussion of the policy-making process.

The problem with the existing approaches to policy making in Japan revealed in this literature are unhelpful in outlining the exact position of business in the policy-making process. We can start, for example, with the often cited notion of a ruling triad, or even iron triangle, of interests in Japan represented by the ruling LDP, the bureaucracy and big business. Even if we accept the idea that these are the predominant actors in Japanese politics, the ruling party and the bureaucracy capture the attention of most analysts. This is true even of studies which try to de-emphasize the powers of the bureaucracy (Samuels, 1987; Uriu, 1996) as they still give the impression that business, even 'big' business, is the weaker of the three even if they maintain control over their own domain.

When discussion moves to a more theoretical level, these problems are compounded. In contrast to the free-for-all of interest group politics in the US, the Japanese system has appeared more ordered in the organisation of interests and the relationship of interests to the state. Thus, attempts to apply theories of 'pluralism' drawn from the US experience were doomed to failure. In an effort to salvage the concept, Muramatsu and Krauss (1987) created the notion of 'patterned pluralism' which gave a greater role to societal and state patterns of interaction than allowed for in the original pluralist theory. However, this notion of patterning leaves open the question of the degree to which interests can be patterned and still be pluralistic.

Bureaucratic context of business politics

This does not mean that comparative benchmarks are meaningless. It is merely suggested that macro-political concepts of regime type must be suspended occasionally. Rather than start with a systemic or structural framework and look for evidence to determine whether or not there is a 'fit' with the theory, it can be argued that a focus on the character and behaviour of actors, or 'agents' in structural terms, is an equally legitimate starting point. This is certainly the way the situation is best understood in Japan. It is no doubt atheoretical, but the focus of much of the practical literature on the interaction of business leaders, senior bureaucrats and politicians focuses on individuals. While a plethora of Japanese names would make any study incomprehensible, specific individuals must be examined to make sense of the political context in which Japanese business operates.

The powers of the Japanese bureaucracy

First, this chapter must address the strong popular perception that the Japanese bureaucracy plays the predominant role in Japanese policy making. This view has been reinforced, if not created, by Chalmers Johnson's study of the role of the MITI in the creation of the Japanese economic miracle (Johnson, 1982). This is a view widely shared by the business community – as evidenced, for example, by a management text by the foremost business publisher in Japan, Nihon Keizai Shimbun, which refers to MITI as Japan's real corporate leaders (Nihon Keizai Shimbun Sha, 1990: 197–200) Even more recent studies have examined the ways in which the powerful Ministry of Finance manipulated politicians in order to realise the implementation of an unpopular new consumption tax in Japan in 1988 (Kato, 1994).

There is a robust literature which opposes this bureaucratic dominance thesis. Richard Samuels' study of the historical development of the energy industry in Japan emphasises not only private sector dynamism but also the failure of the bureaucracy to shape the industry as they would have liked (Samuels, 1987). Even the widely used Nihon Keizai Shimbun textbook points to the classic example of MITI's failure to bring about a merger of Honda and Prince Motors as indicative of the limits of bureaucratic power (Nikkei Keizai Shimbun Sha, 1990: 200). Regardless of whether or not this particular case is significant or not, it would be a mistake to view the bureaucracy as the driving force in the policy-making nexus between business and politics in Japan. Ramseyer and Rosenbluth even go so far as to argue that the politicians are really the principle players but allow the bureaucrats, as agents, leeway in the formulation and implementation of policy (Ramseyer and Rosenbluth, 1993). They insist that 'LDP leaders both set the basic contours of economic regulation and constrain their bureaucratic agents effectively enough so that they can rely on them to perform politically sensitive jobs' (Ibid. 140). The truth is more often between the two extremes of bureaucratic and political control, but the fact is that bureaucrats are involved in questionable arrangements and have benefited from them as much as politicians (Babb, 1995: 546–7).

Therefore, the discussion which follows focuses on the ways in which business influences the policy-making process – sometimes in collusion with bureaucrats – rather than cases of conflict between the bureaucracy and business. Indeed, most of the literature in English on the Japanese bureaucracy is part of a larger debate over the appropriate role of state intervention, and this is not an issue that needs to be discussed here. It merely needs to be noted that Japanese business recognises that the bureaucracy does have important administrative powers which impinge on the interests of business. In fact, one continuing theme of Japanese business leaders is the need for a reduction in the powers of the bureaucracy. This means that some mention has to be made of several aspects of the bureaucracy related to Japanese business even if the focus of this book is business and politicians.

One reason why bureaucrats are considered to be so powerful in Japan is that they have been able to exercise considerable discretion over the implementation of policy. The legislation governing most policy areas in Japan specify little of the detail of implementation and only set out broad guidelines for the application of the law to specific circumstances. In fact, the relevant law for covering a policy domain will often end with the clause that application may be varied at the discretion of the minister responsible. While the minister would be a politician in most cases, this might suggest political control, but few ministers have the energy or expertise to become involved with more than a handful of administrative decisions. Finally, there is little recourse to appeal against administrative decisions in Japan and, of course, this also considerably enhances the powers of the bureaucracy. Should a company choose to use the courts to contest an administrative ruling, the court system in Japan has relatively few judges to hear cases so delays can mean cases are not determined for several years or, in some contentious cases, for decades. Moreover, the

Bureaucratic context of business politics

Japanese courts – appointed by conservative judicial bureaucrats heavily influenced by the LDP – take a very narrow view of their powers of judicial review. As a result, legal challenges to administrative decisions take too long and are rejected by the courts anyway. This makes a such a course of action unprofitable.

It is necessary here to make a distinction between law and 'administrative guidance.' Only the Japanese parliament can pass laws (*horitsu*) but the guidelines to implement a law are left to the cabinet which issues enabling executive directives (*seirei*) with the detailed rules to be applied left to a ministerial directive (*shorei*) issued in the name of the cabinet minister in charge. Each of these three are legally binding. However, ministry officials may issue 'administrative guidance' (*gyosei shido*) providing an interpretation of the legal guidelines for a specific circumstance. These are of three types in descending order of severity: bureau chief notification (*kyokucho tsuchi*), section chief notification (*kacho tsuchi*) and office contact (*jimu renraku*). The first involves an opinion issued by the more powerful bureau chief providing an official opinion on the way in which a law is being intepretated in a given situation. The second does the same but by an individual in the less powerful post of section chief. The last is merely official contact by an agency but is the least formal of the three and the least forceful.

Johnson (1982: 242–74) discusses administrative guidance in his *MITI and the Japanese Miracle* to underline the administrative powers of the Japanese bureaucracy that go beyond the law. Such guidance is not part of the law and a ministry has no legal power to enforce its interpretations, but it is not unknown for a ministry to retaliate against those who ignore such guidance by using its regulatory powers in other areas. Intransigent firms may find that their applications to the ministry which regulates them are delayed or refused, and those ministries with the powers of audit and inspection may take a new interest in a difficult firm. Such activities could be viewed as an abuse of power, but Japanese courts have been slow to recognise such arguments. On the other hand, it has been suggested that there are virtues to administrative guidance in that ministries have the flexibility to adjust implementation of law to fit the circumstances and industry is kept informed of the views of the authorities.

Yet, it has also been argued that there are problems of ministerial complicity in industry collusion and the opportunity for officials to use this guidance for corrupt ends (Shindo, 1990). This negative side was seen in the actions of the securities firms in the early 1990s who were covering the stock market losses of their best customers with Ministry of Finance turning a blind eye to the practice. In addition, the Recruit scandal of the late 1980s implicated officials from a number of agencies in using their regulatory powers for the Recruit company for which they were illegally compensated. More recently, two MOF officials were arrested in January 1998 on suspicion of taking bribes from nearly all of the leading banks in Japan: Sanwa, Asahi, Daiichi Kangyo, Hokkaido Takushoku, Mitsubishi-Tokyo and Sumitomo. The bribes were paid allegedly in exchange for advance warning of ministry inspections. A number of other MOF officials were also disciplined for accepting entertainment from financial institutions in exchange for favourable treatment.

The descent from heaven (*amakudari*)

Another problematic way by which business can maintain knowledge and insight into the bureaucracy and politics is to give jobs to former bureaucrats. The posts are usually at a high level in the company, normally as a member of the board of directors, and the remuneration is generous. In Japanese this is known as *amakudaru*, which literally means 'descent from heaven' based on the old idea that entering the real world of business is a step down from the prestigious role as a top government official. In reality these second careers are very lucrative, and for the majority of officials who are not appointed to senior bureaucratic posts (that is, bureau chief, administrative vice-minister, etc.) and are forced to retire by the age of 55, these jobs are crucial to their financial security.

It is not without good reason that this phenomenon has occupied the attention of many scholars and critics. (Calder, 1989; Nakano, 1998; Schaede, 1995; Usui and Colignon, 1995) However, the problem is that the overall impact of the practice is ambiguous, especially from the point of view of determining whether former bureaucrats impose agency views on industry or retired officials are useful tools by which industry lobbies government agencies. No doubt the influences go both ways. For industry, inside knowledge of the ministry which regulates them and creates the policies which shapes their activities is extremely useful. At the same time, former bureaucrats can shape the industry by allowing them to anticipate strongly held official views and focus on the areas of policy which can reasonably be changed. The

Table 5.1 *Amakudari* destinations of former MOF officials (as of February 1998)

Type of financial institution	Number of former officials	Type of post Director	Auditor
Major Banks (*toshi ginko*)	1	1	–
Long-term Trust Banks	3	1	2
Trust Banks	2	1	1
Regional Banks	42	37	5
Securities Firms	24	10	14
Secondary Regional Banks	70	55	15
Life Insurance Firms	13	8	5
Property Insurance Firms	9	6	3

Source: *Sankei Shimbun*, 18 February 1998.

overall impact, as many have noted, is a closer working relationship between business and the state.

The extent of this practice can be illustrated by the destinations of Ministry of Finance officials. It is significant that relatively few go to the top banks in the country and the largest number are to be found in the regional banks of Japan which are considered to be the least competitive and the most reluctant to permit deregulation of financial services. Other favoured destinations are securities and insurance firms but, again, not the top firms in the industry. Most are given posts as members of the board of directors, including a large number of working directors. The only other type of post was that of auditor (most notably in the securities industry) – which is understandable given their knowledge of relevant regulations (see Table 5.1).

In addition, the MOF, like all other top government agencies, supplies the top personnel for a number of public sector organsations. These would include special corporations (Export–Import Bank of Japan, People's Finance Corporation, Japan Development Bank) as well as a variety of other publicly established organisations, including foundations and research institutes. These special corporations, in particular, can command considerable resources of their own, but all are based on endowments supplied at taxpayers' expense, and make investments, conduct research and publish information all of which have significant public policy implications. Some

Table 5.2 Types of semi-governmental *Amakudari* destinations in 1997

Agency	Special corporations	Special public corporations
Ministry of Finance	3	810
Ministry of Construction	8	339
Ministry of Agriculture	9	494
Ministry of Transport	9	853
Ministry of Posts and Telecommunications	2	225
Minstry of Health and Welfare	6	575
Ministry of International Trade and Industry	14	909
Science and Technology Agency	5	125
Land Agency	3	41
Economic Planning Agency	2	30
Environment Agency	2	66
Hokkaido Development Agency	1	9
Okinawa Development Agency	1	3
General Affairs Agency	1	31
Defence Agency	–	23
Police Agency	–	51
Ministry of Foreign Affairs	2	244
Ministry of Labour	6	442
Ministry of Education	8	1,802
Home Ministry	2	74

Source: Civil Watch, 1999, website.

play a role in training and regulation in the relevant industry. Each of Japan's ministries and agencies maintain links to their associated organisations, through *amakudari* and also the secondment of current agency officials. Private sector firms can also often second their own employees (often as 'researchers') to these organisations to establish contacts and keep abreast of policy trends. The number of such organisations provides an important pool of *amakudari* destinations (see Table 5.2).

As a result of *amakudari*, Japanese officials have extensive influence, not only at the heart of the firm itself, but also in the numerous semi-governmental agencies and quangos which regulate and monitor each industry. At the same time, there are advantages to the firms which participate in such a system as it provides useful inside information and allows firms the opportunity to monitor and anticipate trends in regulations and policy making. The implicit assumption of discussions of *amakudari* is that the presence of former officials either extends bureaucratic control into the private sector or that it creates the potential for corruption. Both of these effects can be seen. Nonetheless, it is the informational aspect of these links which firms find valuable and why the practice will not soon disappear.

Controlling and feeding information

Another channel of contact between business and the bureaucracy are both ordinary channels of information exchange and influence, and the more infrequent government commissions discussed in detail below. There is frequent contact between the leadership of major business organisations and senior bureaucrats. The submission of information and policy proposals by such business organisations as Keidanren, Keizai Doyukai and the Japan Chamber of Commerce and Industry are sometimes solicited and sometimes not. There is little doubt that organised business has privileged access to the highest echelons of government.

One of the key means of influence by business in the policy process is through government commissions (*shingikai*). These commissions are created in response to difficult issues which confront widespread or deep-rooted societal concern. They are composed of individuals from a range of occupational groups which vary to some degree according to the issue. Along with academics, however, most incorporate business leaders who can give an air of respectability and authority to the deliberations. Indeed, government commissions are one of the key ways in which the business community maintains a high public profile.

This was particularly apparent in the Second Ad Hoc Commission on Administrative Reform which had a highly political origin. Although the impetus for this commission can be found in MOF concerns over the fiscal crisis created by the first oil crisis and the subsequent slow growth of the late 1980s, it was the former Prime

Minister, Yasuhiro Nakasone, who used the issue to build his stature in the party and provide a focus for his administration. Administrative reform in this context was directed at reducing government costs by such means as the privatisation of Japan's debt-ridden national rail service. Moreover, it also destroyed the power base of one of the most militant Japanese public employees unions which was a convenient side effect for the right-wing Nakasone. The commission also laid the ground work for the privatisation of Japan's telecommunications monopoly, NTT, and the Japan Tobacco and Salt Monopoly. However, the success of the commission is attributed in large part to the leadership of the commission chair, Toshio Doko, former chair of Keidanren and president of Toshiba. Indeed, business leaders invariably play a key role in government commissions.

Nonetheless, the bureaucracy still has the upper hand in this aspect of the policy-making process. An in-depth study of such commissions by Schwartz (1998) amply documents the extent to which the parent agencies of such commissions (that is, bureaucratic agencies) are able to control and manipulate them. While nominally independent of the bureaucracy, the staff of the commission secretariat are supplied by the relevant agency and much of the information presented to the commission is provided by the staff of the agency concerned. Moreover, the commissions report directly to the agency and it is the bureaucrats who decide whether to take action on a commission report or how to implement it if they do take action (ibid.: 75–93). Schwartz's conclusions are muddled, however, by the fact that he is supports a neo-pluralist view of Japan defined as the situation in which 'small and fairly stable sets of well-organised, narrowly focused state and societal actors dominate relatively self-contained policy domains by privatising conflicts and resorting to informal decision making' (ibid.: 284). However, he goes on to admit that 'Japanese neo-pluralism is most often bureaucratically led: the compartmentalisation of policy domains follows the lines of ministerial jurisdiction, and agency officials are frequently able to adjust conflicts in a deliberate, self-interested way' (ibid.). 'Nevertheless,' he concludes, 'Japanese bureaucrats exercise power most frequently and effectively via, in cooperation with politicians and private actors, rather than vis-à-vis, in control of them, and when bureaucratic jurisdiction is divided or when policies are strongly distributive in nature, then politicians will play a more prominent role' (ibid.).

Simply put, Japanese bureaucrats have the upper hand in areas

Bureaucratic context of business politics

of their specific policy responsibility, but this does not mean that private actors cannot get their way so long as agency interests are taken into account in any proposed changes. Indeed, business has been very successful at taking advantage of commissions, in contrast to organised labour for example, precisely because it has been able to lobby the bureaucracy and LDP politicians beyond simple membership on commissions. Moreover, business has clearly defined sectoral interests which – more often than not – can be accommodated within a ministerial policy domain. It is only in areas of deregulation and the transformation or reduction of ministerial powers where political allies have become crucial.

The political involvements of the Japanese bureaucracy

The political nature of Japanese bureaucrats was made openly obvious when the anti-LDP coalition of 1993–94 collapsed. The influence of bureaucrats had noticeably increased during the anti-LDP Hosokawa government, especially in ministries where an inexperienced politician had been made minister. At the same time, one of the key leaders of the coalition, Ichiro Ozawa, and his supporters had begun to try to sever the links between LDP-friendly politicians and the bureaucracy. Ozawa knew from his own cultivation of sympathetic bureaucrats that officials could leak information and obstruct policy as well as help design and implement policy, so he was careful to keep an eye on intra-bureaucratic politics. Moreover, Ozawa-friendly bureaucrats expected to reap the benefits of their mentor being in office as it might help them reach the highest levels of the bureaucracy, especially important bureau chief and administrative vice-minister roles which are not decided purely on seniority.

Controversy erupted, however, when the MITI minister in the Hosokawa cabinet, Hiroshi Kumagai – himself a former MITI official – requested and received the resignation of Industrial Policy Bureau chief, Masahisa Naito, in December 1993 for giving a promotion to MITI official on what appeared to be political grounds. The promoted official had run as an LDP candidate in the 1993 general election and it was alleged that Naito had given the promotion in an attempt to boost the candidate's standing with the electorate. This was the first time an MITI official had ever been openly called upon to resign, and the suspicion was that Ozawa was trying to remould the bureaucracy according to his preferences and weed out LDP influences. By May

1994, the incident was being used by the LDP to attack Kumagai, then the Chief Cabinet Secretary, for blatant political interference in the bureaucracy. In fact, the issue of bureaucratic advance had always been political in some respects and the fall of the LDP government merely made it more apparent. The fear was that should the LDP return to power, those bureaucrats who had helped the coalition might be punished in turn.

Once the LDP was back in power, however, initial retribution against bureaucrats who had helped their enemies was minor. Only the Finance Ministry administrative vice-minister, Jiro Saito, and MITI administrative vice-minister, Hideaki Kumano, were singled out as having been too close to the anti-LDP government and dismissed. Indeed, all potentially politically motivated dismissals were similarly limited to the vice-minister class, and change of that post was to be expected with any change of government. Nonetheless, LDP ministers made no secret of their desire to return to things as they had been in the past. Transport Minister, Shizuka Kamei, even went so far as to tell a meeting of senior ministry bureaucrats: 'The Transport Ministry is too close to the Japan Renewal Party [one of the key anti-LDP coalition parties]. I would like to see you return to your previous position' in a reference to the strong past ties of the ministry to the Mitsuzuka faction (Suzuki, 1995: 310–11). Even so, it took considerable effort for one division chief in the ministry, Mitsuo Igarashi, seen as tied to Ozawa to lose the taint of the link (*Foresight*, January 1995: 119). As a result, bureaucrats drifted into a role as coordinators rather than political players. Despite the mountain of difficult tasks facing them, the administrative vice-minister became 'accomodationist' rather than proactive, even in the more politicised ministries such as the MOF and MITI (*Yomiuri Shimbun*, 22 June 1995).

By the following year, the LDP had decided to make the powers of the bureaucracy an issue and this further weakened the position of Japanese bureaucrats. The declared aim of the new cabinet of Ryotaro Hashimoto in the wake of the LDP's victory in the 1996 general election was to pursue so-called 'administrative reform'. Even before the election, this was the issue which politicians in all parties were claiming as their own, though the exact meaning of the term varied dramatically from politician to politician. The main thread in the concept, however, was a desire to limit the powers of the bureaucracy. The motives and consequences of these changes will be examined after the involvement of politicians in the policy-making process is considered.

Conclusions

This chapter has examined the powers of the bureaucracy and the extent of bureaucratic influence, and it has found that these remain formidable despite the important changes in the past few years. *Amakudari* has been limited, restrictions on entertainment of bureaucrats are in place and the powers of the bureaucracy are being delimited as their agencies are being reorganised and downsized. Even so, one might question the degree to which this will have an effect on actual behaviour. For evidence of the impact (or lack of impact) of recent reforms, one need only look at the questions raised in 1999 about the entertainment of Ministry of Agriculture officials and the subsequent effect on their choices of *amakudari* posts the following year.

The key point to the above discussion was to assess the widely held view that policy making in Japan is dominated by inscrutable, super-efficient bureaucrats whose tentacles extend into industry itself. In reality, it is difficult to specify the interests of bureaucrats themselves distinct from their attempts to manage conflicting pressures from industry, foreign governments and changes in the marketplace. Current proposals for the reform of Japanese administration will not change the nature of the existing role of the bureaucracy. In fact, the smaller size and rationalising of regulations might even promote an even stronger sense of *esprit de corps*, but no more or less influence. This will be explored further later.

As this chapter has tried to show, so long as the bureaucracy has a policy-making and political role, industries are going to want to have access to bureaucrats to shape policies to suit their interests. Of course, the bureaucrats need to keep in contact with industry as well to ensure effective policy. This ambiguity caused by the policy-making and political nature of the current role of the bureaucracy could only be addressed by transferring more policy-making and political roles to politicians. This leads to the question of the policy-making role of politicians, which is the main focus of the next chapter.

6
Political leadership and policy tribes

The preceding discussion of the powers of the state bureaucracy in Japan is missing an important element in the intermediation of the interests of business: the role of politicians. Politicians provide the crucial link between the demands of business and the requirements of the bureaucracy. They do this in two ways. First, political vision is needed to creatively smooth the way between the narrow legalistic psychology of bureaucrats and the gain-driven orientation of business. Second, politicians can make themselves useful to business in a way that brings elected officials political funding and opportunities to advance their careers. In fact, it is these activities which justify the political contributions made by business to politicians.

Bureaucrats in Japan may have power, but they lack the vision provided by politicians. This was said to me several times by senior Japanese bureaucrats themselves. By this they meant that only politicians can provide the political vision and will to create policy initiatives. These initiatives may be altered by bureaucrats and implemented in ways congenial to bureaucratic requirements but the political vision which starts the process is something that only emerges from the political process. Such political vision has an ideological and social dimension which goes beyond purely an instrumental attitude to the policy process, though particularistic gain business derives from the resultant policies can reinforce the desire to pursue the vision in the first place.

Politicians' 'service' to business is, in contrast, more instrumental. Politicians can protect and extend the interests of firms and business associations which go beyond what bureaucrats do with their control of the minutiae of administrative regulation. Indeed, politicians can challenge, to a degree, the powers of the bureaucracy. Moreover, through the cultivation of knowledge of a policy domain

Political leadership and policy tribes 81

and connections with the bureaucracy, politicians not only make themselves useful to business but also promote their own career. These politicians are the policy 'tribe' (*zoku*) MPs at the core of the Japanese policy-making process.

There is a downside to the policies created by the vision of politicians. They can be used by those who pursue only instrumental gain in a variety of ways ranging from clear corruption to opportunistic exploitation. The bundle of policies which created the bubble economy in Japan was the outgrowth of a series of visionary initiatives to deal with a variety of problems facing the economy in a way which also benefited entrepreneurs. However, the opportunities created were used by criminal elements and others in ways which led to corruption in officialdom, politics and mainstream business. A review of the current state of the politicians in policy tribes and the most recent initiatives of political leaders suggests that the policy-making process still holds the danger of problems not dissimilar to those of the bubble economy.

Policy leadership

Minoru Nakano in his *The Policy-making Process in Contemporary Japan* (1997: 64–102) makes a useful attempt to classify the fundamental patterns of policy making in Japan. He identifies six types of influence on the policy process: government executive politics, *Nagatacho* politics, Diet politics, elite accomodation politics, client-oriented politics and public opinion politics (ibid.: 65). However, these patterns might be simplified further into three groups:

1   interest service
2   agenda-setting initiative
3   bureaucratic parochialism.

The last of these three, bureaucratic parochialism, was dealt with in the previous chapter. This type of policy making only assumes a leadership role when there is a gap between the bureaucratic imperatives of the agencies and policy-making reality, in which case officials attempt to force through initiatives to reduce the gap. A good example would be the MOF and its obsession with Japanese fiscal deficits. It was MOF bureaucrats who did the most to keep the issue on the political agenda and pursue ways of either cutting spending or raising taxes. While a few politicians were eager to make an alliance with

MOF for their own reasons, most resisted spending cuts or new taxes. The only major successes of the MOF came when they allied with Nakasone's administrative reform initiative aimed in part at weakening the left, and with Takeshita who wanted a new tax to finance his own spending schemes.

This suggests that the main policy-making initiatives come from senior politicians. Indeed, all new Japanese Prime Ministers start their administrations by outlining the key goals of their government. These goals normally number about three but one among them is a priority initiative. In the case of Prime Minister Yasuhiro Nakasone in 1982, it was administrative reform – a subject with which he had become familiar and which made him prominent in the years prior to his assumption of power. For his successor in 1987, Prime Minister Noboru Takeshita, the theme was local renewal which meant revitalisation of local areas but was also tied to his efforts to pass a consumption tax to pay for local development schemes. Prime Minister Keizo Obuchi in 1998 chose economic revitalisation and financial system stability – not surprising given the continuing economic downturn in Japan and the near collapse of the financial system. His successor, Prime Minister Yoshiro Mori in 2000, toyed with several ideas before settling on the information technology revolution as we shall see below.

Even those who argue that politicians are constrained by political organisation (factions and the party) acknowledge the 'agenda-setting' role of the Prime Minister (Ramseyer and Rosenbluth, 1997: 64). It is true that some politicians seem to have no policies – such as Prime Minister Eisaku Sato, who has the record for holding office and was jokingly referred to as 'no policy Sato' (*Musaku Sato*) – but even he pushed forward several major initiatives, the most notable being his successful efforts to have Okinawa returned to Japan from US administration (cf. ibid.: 208, n. 6).

There are two mitigating points which need to be made about this agenda-setting power. The first is that the agenda can become a political minefield which can be used for and against competing leaders. The second is that the themes chosen are often ones which require a degree of political concensus to achieve. An example of the first problem can be seen at the start of the administration of Prime Minister Kiichi Miyazawa in 1991 who took the theme of peace keeping, but his adoption of the scheme was foisted on him by the faction leaders who made his administration possible. Indeed,

Political leadership and policy tribes

Miyazawa was put in office after the previous Prime Minister, Toshiki Kaifu's administration theme of political reform (1989–91) was sabotaged by other political leaders in the LDP. This is the *Nagatacho* politics which Nakano gives as one of his patterns of policy making – Nagatacho referring to the political district in Japan equivalent to Westminister in the UK or 'inside the beltway' in Washington, DC (Nakano, 1997: 77–80). *Nagatacho* politics is important but I would place it as a subgroup of the main types.

For the most part, however, these initiatives do tend to acheive change. The process by which they do so is one of establishing a concensus that something in general needs to be done in relation to the problem – the establishment of an ambiguous vision which is difficult to oppose. This concensus then commits other politicians to making progress with the problem and forces them to compromise on issues which they would have otherwise refused to even discuss. Of course, this compromise means that accommodation is necessary, as it is in each of the types of policy patterns. Political leaders must create new schemes, buy off opposition with compensation and engage in log-rolling to balance competing interests. Indeed, many of the initiatives are simply disguised attempts to finesse opposition from entrenched interests by cajoling them into a compromise. This can be demonstrated in the case of the 'bubble economy' and is also behind a more recent Japanese government initiative on information technology.

These cases lead us to the final type of policy making: interest service. Interestingly, Nakano places the policy 'tribes' (*zoku*) as part of *Nagatacho* politics, and in so much as they can be a part of the political contest between party leaders this is correct. However, it would be simpler and more accurate to put them more fully in his category of client-oriented politics (which he does to a degree). The political and policy activities of MPs on behalf of specific interests, in particular, business interests, is the complete opposite of the role of politicians as visionaries and mediators between interests and agencies. Here the politicians take sides and pursue the interests of narrow groups. This type of interest politics in Japan, as in any other country, causes the most concern and is easily misunderstood. Therefore, a full discussion of the purest manifestation of interest politics, the phenomena of policy tribes is required.

Policy tribes (*zoku*)

Japanese politicians have been constantly derided for their lack of policy competence. Japan's financial daily, the *Nihon Keizai Shimbun*, has even argued that 'Bureaucratic power has its origins in the poor quality of politicians' (*The Nikkei Weekly*, 17 January 1994). However, this lack of knowledge of policy began to be remedied to a degree by the emergence of so-called policy tribes in the 1980s. *Zoku* MPs specialise in a given policy area and cultivate bureaucratic expertise in that area through experience in related posts in the LDP and the government. They use their specialist knowledge and connections to bring concrete benefits to their constituents and to their business supporters, as well as raise funds and mobilise resources from the industries connected with the policy area. As a result, they are found to be useful to their faction leader who promotes them to more prestigious and powerful posts. As a result, policy competence in the LDP was and is a by-product of the efforts of individual MPs to advance their careers.

It is important here, however, to stress that this not, as widely argued, simply a matter of seniority. Following from Sato and Matsuzaki, a number of political scientists have imagined an idealised career path for LDP politicians (see Table 6.1). It starts in the MP's first term with membership on a committee of the LDP's Political Affairs Research Committee (PARC) which considers LDP policy and related legislation. After the next election, an MP can rise to act as a secretary for a parliamentary committee, become a vice-chair of a PARC committee or even act as a political vice-minister to a government ministry. By a third term in office, the MP can become a full-fledged chair of a PARC committee with some influence over a particular area of policy. By the fourth or fifth term, there are opportunities to act as a party vice-secretary helping to manage party affairs or director of an LDP bureau with substantive responsibilities in the party (including overall coordination of policy). Finally, after six terms or more in parliament, an MP can obtain the most coveted position of cabinet minister. All this suggests a clear career path to political power in Japan based on seniority.

In fact, however, there is no such thing as simple seniority. Obviously those elected fewer times would have fewer chances to assume posts, but the potential pool from which ever more powerful politicians could be drawn was always limited and advancement to senior levels of the party was not based on seniority. That is, it was not

Table 6.1 A 'typical' career path of a Liberal Democratic Party MP

Term in office	Party or government post
1st term	LDP Political Affairs Research Committee (PARC) member
2nd term	Parliamentary committee secretary Vice-chair of a PARC committee Political vice-minister
3rd term	PARC committee chair
4th term or 5th term	Party vice-secretary Director of a LDP bureau
6th term or more	Cabinet post

Sources: Kohno, 1997: 95; Ramseyer and Rosenbluth,1993: 86; Sato and Matsuzaki, 1986: 39.

just a matter of acquiring a curriculum vitae full of posts. Instead, it has become increasingly important for ambitious politicians to show their knowledge of a given policy area to the benefit of their faction leaders and the businesses with an interest in the policy domain. Such politicians advanced more rapidly and acquired the most desirable posts which were, after all, limited in number, and therefore could not be held by all LDP MPs even given a particularly long career (that is, if re-elected many times).

In all of the schemes to identify *zoku* MPs, the greatest weight is given to the career paths with those holding the largest number of key posts responsible for a given policy area. Obviously, an MP who has been involved with policy making in a specific area over a number of years will develop some competence in the policy domain. They can use this knowledge to approach the bureaucracy and negotiate on behalf of specific interest groups or businesses. Indeed, bureaucrats consider *zoku* MPs a nuisance because they can authoritatively interfere with the bureaucracy. In theory, the parliament is sovereign over the governmental agencies. In reality, bureaucrats have many means to exercise control, as we have seen in the previous chapter. *Zoku* MPs go some way towards redressing the balance back in favour of the parliament, though admittedly only for the narrow interests which they represent.

One special group of *zoku* MPs are those MPs who are former bureaucrats. These former officials have useful and detailed inside knowledge of governmental agencies and policies. *Zoku* rating schemes are that former bureaucratic experience is weighted heavily as evidence of *zoku* status. This assumes that they are acting on behalf of the party and its constituent interest. However, as we have seen with *amakudari*, there is no guarantee of the direction in which a former bureaucrat might exert influence. Moreover, recent evidence (see next chapter) suggests that they are less interested in their former official domains than rating schemes might suggest.

The phenomena of *zoku* MPs occupies a large amount of the discussion in this chapter precisely because it is so important to the role played by politicians in relation to business interests. This is no more obvious than in recent attempts at regulatory reform. Any proposals for reform legislation must work their way through the relevant committees of the LDP, but two deliberation rules mean that it is easy to block the progress of new legislation. According to a former LDP MP, these two rules are that any LDP MPs has an unlimited right to speak at these meetings and unanimity is required for a proposal to pass the committee (Kurimoto, 1999: 195–201). Therefore, it takes only a few *zoku* MPs to retard change (that is, protect vested interests) by use of their filibustering rights. This largely explains the difficulties for the LDP in taking the initiative in economic reform.

While only a handful of *zoku* MPs can have a profound impact, the fact is all of the most powerful leading factions specialise in particular policy domains making the deep rooted problem of entrenched interests even worse by assuring that any legislative proposals that do emerge are aimed at enhancing particularly interests. Iwai and Inoguchi's (1987) study of the *zoku* phenomena concentrates on eleven main areas of activity: commerce, agriculture, fisheries, transport, construction, welfare, labour, education, posts and telecommunications, finance and defence. While the distribution of *zoku* expertise across factions in the LDP was uneven, the study clearly demonstrates the ability of the Tanaka faction to dominate the most lucrative *zoku* niches. All other factions have been keen to imitate the Tanaka faction and provide their own expertise in defence of special interests.

As Table 6.2 shows, the Tanaka faction dominated the construction and telecommunications *zoku*, but also had a strong presence in commerce, transport, welfare, finance and defence. To a degree, this is a function of size: the Tanaka faction is the largest while the Komoto faction and MPs not affiliated to a faction are relatively few in number.

Political leadership and policy tribes 87

Table 6.2 *Zoku* MPs and factions (both Upper and Lower House MPs) in 1985

	Tanaka	Miyazawa	Nakasone	Abe	Komoto	None
Commerce	34.1	14.6	26.8	22.0	2.4	0.0
Agriculture	13.5	16.2	29.7	21.6	13.5	5.4
Fisheries	11.1	44.4	22.0	0.0	11.1	11.1
Transport	28.0	8.0	16.0	36.0	8.0	4.0
Construction	68.0	15.6	9.4	3.1	0.0	3.1
Welfare	29.2	37.5	12.5	16.7	4.2	0.0
Labour	16.7	38.7	22.2	16.7	5.6	0.0
Education	9.5	0.0	33.3	23.8	19.0	14.3
Communications	56.3	12.5	6.3	12.5	12.5	0.0
Finance	22.7	31.8	18.2	22.7	4.5	0.0
Defence	28.6	9.5	14.3	33.3	4.8	9.5

Source: Iwai and Inoguchi, 1987: 150.
Note: All figures are percentages of total *zoku* MPs but they may not add up to 100 per cent due to rounding.

Nonetheless, the Tanaka faction was not much larger than its three main rivals – the factions of Miyazawa, Nakasone and Abe.

The widespread involvement of all factions in commerce, agriculture and transport is an indication of the gains to be made for local constituencies and individual MPs from policy knowledge of these areas. Less lucrative areas of *zoku* activity, such as welfare, education or labour, on the other hand, are motivated by other factors – such as right-wing ideology in the case of the Nakasone faction's interest in education. Not surprisingly, the weakest faction, that of Toshio Komoto, was also the least involved in *zoku* politics.

The Tanaka faction's connections with the construction and postal service (communications) were the most lucrative of the *zoku* networks. Construction has been an ideal sector since policy decisions about the scale, location and contracting of public works projects can often be influenced by policy decisions in which construction *zoku* can become involved. Indeed, it was usual practice for construction companies to reward the Tanaka faction a percentage of a public works contract as a kickback for getting the project approved. The bubble economy of the late 1980s saw this pattern of political business relations expand throughout Japan beyond the Tanaka faction.

A case study of politics and interest politics at work: the bubble economy

The bubble economy was an extension of Tanaka-style politics on a large scale. In this case study, we can see the interaction of the politics of accommodation with policy business initiatives. The combination of the two produced an artificial economic bubble which was profitable for firms and politicians but ended in extensive and long-term damage to the Japanese economy.

The starting point for the bubble was the very understandable concern of the Japanese government for the ability of industry to adjust to appreciation of the value of the yen after the Louvre and Plaza accords in the mid-1980s. In order to permit Japanese industry to relocate its low-wage manufacturing overseas, mainly to Southeast Asia, and create new higher value-added enterprises to re-employ displaced workers, the Bank of Japan set interest rates very low – with an adjustment for inflation, effectively zero or less than zero. Firms did transfer production overseas and create new enterprises, but the availability of, effectively, free money fuelled speculation in real estate and the accumulation of massive corporate debt backed by artificially inflated assets.

Several policy initiatives expanded the bubble even further. One key initiative was the law to encourage the development of 'leisure' facilities in an effort to respond to foreign criticism that Japanese employees work too long hours and have no opportunities for leisure pursuits (Itagaki, 1987: 181–200). This resulted in the passage of a law in the last days of the Nakasone administration in 1987 giving favourable tax treatment and other encouragement to the development of such facilities. It is important to note, however, that the major proponents were members of the Takeshita (former Tanaka) faction, such as Keizo Obuchi. In fact, Obuchi was identified at the time as one of the new 'leisure *zoku*'. In keeping with the construction industry policy predominance and rural development orientation of the Tanaka-Takeshita faction, the law had the additional advantage of encouraging construction projects in rural areas, especially the use of agriculturally unproductive land for golf courses. Indeed, the Takeshita administration slogan of local renewal included the notion of development projects such as these. Moreover, the policies had an expansionary effect as land prices rose and everyone joined to gain from the development boom. Even golf course club memberships – extremely expensive in Japan – were floated on financial exchanges to provide further capital and produced a bubble market of their own.

Yet, it was not just construction and related business which gained from these policies. This environment was also exploited by Japanese organised crime (*yakuza*). The *yakuza* were especially active in these leisure developments and other similar projects. They borrowed large sums, raised further finance through sales of memberships and equity shares, and then the money disappeared and the projects eventually ground to a halt. It is estimated that more than 40 per cent of the unrecoverable bad loans held by financial institutions in the current economic crisis in Japan can be traced back to the *yakuza* (*Yomiuri Shimbun*, 31 March 1999).

This might seem an unfortunate by-product of the bubble economy, but it is important to realise how the *yakuza* were an integral part of the bubble and deeply involved both with politicians and major firms in Japan. Moreover, gangsterism has a long association with the construction industry and the property market, which were at the centre of the bubble economy, and has connections to most LDP constituency support organisations. We have already seen how organised crime was used by Takeshita to solve his own political problems. For business, *yakuza* or their imitators were useful is enforcing illegal bid-rigging agreements and kickbacks to politicians. They could also engage in intimidation to force landowners to sell land for large-scale redevelopment projects or remove tenants protected by a Japanese legal system which – at the time – provided extensive rights for those who rent.

Many of these practices were widespread and well-known, but were only considered a problem once financial institutions began to collapse. One prominent case as early as 1995 involved the Tokyo Kyowa Credit Association and Anzen Credit Bank which exposed the murky world of bubble finance. After weeks of investigation, three former credit union executives and the president of a related company were arrested on 27 June 1995 for arranging illegal loans which caused the collapse of these two financial bodies. The total of bad loans exceeded 110 billion yen and were initially related to golf course and resort development companies, including some that received financing before local government planning approval had been obtained, though most of the projects were never initiated. In addition, there was insufficient collateral pledged for the loans so the prospects for recovery of the debt was small.

The case had a political dimension as the former Minister of Labour, Toshio Yamaguchi, and a former Director General of the Defence Agency, Keisuke Nakanishi, as well as a senior bureaucrat in the Minister of Finance, Hiroaki Taya, were implicated in the scandal. Yamaguchi's brother was a member of the board of directors of a country club with ties to the golf course development scheme and the minister had acted as a joint surety on the loan. Nakanishi admitted renting an apartment from the former president of Tokyo Kyowa Credit, Harunori Takahashi, and acknowledged that a related firm had purchased 60 million yen of political reception tickets from him but denied he had done anything illegal or unethical. The bureaucrat Taya received a trip to Hong Kong on Takahashi's private airplane, but as he had no direct responsibility for banking supervision at any time, he was only reprimanded. In fact, politicians and bureaucrats were implicated, but none were arrested.

This was not just an isolated incident, as nearly all Japanese financial institutions were involved in such deals, either directly, or indirectly though the supply of funds to dubious financial institutions. Indeed, most politicians have connections to similar projects throughout Japan, including the winner of the 1999 leadership election of the main opposition Demcratic Party, Yukio Hatoyama, who was implicated in a dubious development scheme in his constituency in 1991 (though at the time he was still an LDP MP) (Ito, 1996: 200–6).

The key point is that both politicians and banks knew what was happening and were enmeshed in the world being created by these policies even if they tried to distance themselves from the more shadowy corners of that world. The problem spread from the banks throughout the entire corporate sector. Many major Japanese firms currently have debt problems because of dubious investments in land and property development or because they are caught in the spiral of debt with those who were entangled in financing the bubble encouraged by aggressive lending strategies of financial institutions. Politicians were involved directly as facilitators or indirectly through policy initiatives around which many schemes were based. The policy created the context in which questionable practices could flourish and, since politicians and established businesses were often the direct and indirect beneficiaries of these schemes, their support is not surprising.

Political leadership and policy tribes

Conclusions

In this chapter the focus of discussion of policy making shifted away from the bureaucracy to politicians. The phenomenon of *zoku* demonstrates that politicians do play a key role in interest intermediation and policy making. This role continues to grow and seems set to expand even further under the new government restructuring. Therefore, *zoku* MPs are important to any industry for their knowledge of and contact with the bureaucracy.

At the same time, the *zoku* deal with only the small picture. The policy agenda is set at the highest levels of the government and provides the truly dramatic initiatives which can be colonised by business interests. This was true of the bubble economy and will no doubt be true of the Mori administration's 'IT 2000' initiative if it unfolds along the historical pattern. That is why this chapter reiterated the story of the bubble economy as it provides lessons still relevant to Japan. Bubble politics and policies profoundly influenced the corporate strategies of firms – both in the context of the policies that created it and in the legacy it left behind.

Yet despite the serious consequences of the bubble, neither LDP policy making nor corporate strategy has changed. Public works, and recent related programmes, are intended to stimulate the Japanese economy, but end up reinforcing patterns of political and social behaviour associated with corruption and organised crime in the past. There is little evidence that anything has changed in this respect despite superficial changes in other areas. Indeed, the rise of a new economy holds the danger of merely creating new opportunities for political business and policy business entrepreneurs which will mean further corruption scandals and collusive behaviour.

7

The changing institutional structure of business interest politics

While the general principles of bureaucratic and *zoku* politics revealed in the two previous chapters continue to apply, there have been dramatic changes in the institutional structure of the Japanese government starting with a total reorganisation of the central bureaucracy and cabinet in January 2001. This chapter will assess these changes in light of existing practice and the current evidence for continuity and change.

The changes to the bureaucracy were made possible by a series of serious scandals involving nearly all of the key government agencies since 1995. They started with an HIV-tainted blood scandal and were followed by widespread allegations of corruption in the powerful MOF based on public exposure of the practices of MOF–financial institution relations. The aims of the reforms were to reduce the powers of the bureaucracy and cut the cost of government. Politicians also found the issue politically useful for diverting public attention away from political corruption.

Yet, the new reforms also have implication for politicians. Some of the reforms are aimed at increasing the policy competence of politicians to compensate for a reduced role for bureaucrats. However, these reforms will not reduce the tendency for *zoku* MPs to dominate the policy-making process and may actually increase their influence. The evidence for the lack of change in this area is presented in the context of a discussion of public works and the Mori government initiative to promote an information technology (IT) revolution in Japan. In any case, these changes will at least have an impact on the policy environment in which business operates in Japan.

Scandal and the attack on bureaucratic power

The attack on bureaucratic power began in earnest after the LDP victory in the October 1996 general election. Even prior to the election the bureaucracy faced increasing public criticism for its poor handling of a number of issues, most notably the housing loan corporation crisis and the HIV scandal, the latter of which led to the arrest of a former Health Ministry section chief charged with improper conduct. In fact, anti-bureaucratic sentiment might explain why former bureaucrats did so poorly in the October 1996 election. Normally, ambitious senior bureaucrats ran for office as a second career once they reached retirement age. Most ran as LDP candidates and most were successful. But 1996 was different. Partly this lack of success candidates can be blamed on an increase in the number of candidates running for parties other than the LDP, but even LDP candidates failed to be elected. In fact, out of thirty-nine former bureaucrat candidates running, only twelve were elected. Worst hit were former MOF candidates with only one out of nine elected, but even former Construction Ministry candidates only saw one out of seven gain office.

After the election, an unusual scandal involving the Welfare Ministry dominated the headlines. While opportunities for illicit gain have always been present in the relationship between bureaucrats and industry in construction or finance, the Welfare Ministry was not usually associated with lucrative contracts or policy changes with substantial rewards for individual firms. Yet, the former administrative vice-minister of the Welfare Ministry, Nobuhara Okamitsu, was charged with accepting a 65 million yen bribe over subsidies for the construction of special care facilities for the elderly and disabled. In a way, the scandal indicated the change in the orientation of public policy which had occurred under the Hosokawa and Murayama governments. These new-style government had placed more emphasis on the general provision of social services, particularly those available in urban areas, whereas the LDP had in the past used agricultural subsidies or public works to achieve similar aims but to the advantage of rural areas. The shift from agriculture and public works construction to welfare provision did nothing, however, to diminish corruption – it merely created new opportunities for graft in new areas.

Though administrative reform was not focused entirely on addressing bureaucratic corruption, the scandals gave the reforms additional impetus. In a way, however, it hardly mattered. It was difficult to identify exactly what was the focus of administrative reform because it included a plethora of disparate issues. Marginal changes to the organization and even the size of the bureaucracy were being advocated, and some regulations were likely to be modified to appease public opinion. Even so, proposals for change in 1996 which would have an impact on major business interests were couched in vague language, and one of the most important proposals – a reduction in the public works budget – had already been rejected out of hand by the LDP. The link between entrenched economic interests, the bureaucracy and the LDP could not be broken so easily.

It was the financial scandals involving the powerful MOF in 1998, noted above, which had the biggest impact on the relationship between business and the bureaucracy. This scandal highlighted the extent to which leading businesses had close personal contact with senior bureaucrats. While the impetus for change was a scandal involving payment for information related to the regulatory role of the ministry, a great deal of the contact by business with the bureaucracy dealt with policy and political matters. Indeed, since senior bureaucrats were so deeply involved with politicians and were very knowledgeable in the policy areas of interest to the business they regulated, it was not strange that business sought out bureaucratic views on key policy and political issues.

The importance of this type of information is well-attested by the book *MOF Tan no Kokuhaku* (Confessions of an MOF Handler) (Okura, 1996) in which the senior employee of a major Japanese bank published his notes on his dealings with the ministry as the one responsible for the relationship with MOF. The book, published in 1996 and believed to be part of the impetus for investigations into the ministry, relates stories of luxury meals costing 300,000 yen, golf outings, gifts including cash up to 1 million yen, and even the provision of sex to MOF officials. Yet, more than the lurid details of the widespread scandal – many officials were involved beyond those prosecuted – the book is interesting for the defence it makes of the need for this type of work.

The author refers to those responsible for MOF relations as the 'CIA of a bank'. They needed to use various means to gain information because of the importance of MOF for the industry. Nearly all aspects of banking have been heavily regulated by the ministry, and the ministry is deeply involved in all aspects of financial and fiscal policy. As the author puts it: 'Of course, the job of a MOF relations officer was not just to listen to their opinions, all kinds of requests

The changing institutional structure

were made and mutual adjustments made to policies' (Okura, 1996: 26). Given the scope of bureaucratic discretion, lobbying must be directed at the bureaucrats rather than politicians.

While the case of MOF may be seen as an aberration, the fact of the regulatory and policy-making powers of Japan's ministries does mean that industry must understand the opinions and inner working of the bureaucracy. This need explains the extensive publishing industry in Japan dedicated to inside information on bureaucracies, individual bureaucrats and the relationship between bureaucrats and politicians. Promotions and policy statements of career bureaucrats at all levels are followed closely with any changes in patterns or open disputes carefully noted. Insider magazines such as *Foresight* and *Sentaku* provide a regular supply of this information to business readers. This obsession with bureaucratic politics which can be gleaned from the daily newspapers, especially the *Nihon Keizai Shimbun* (the *Wall Street Journal* or *Financial Times* equivalent in Japan). Finally, there are books and other monographs which provide gossip and analysis of the ministries, and some even devoted to particular bureaus within ministries. This is one reason those involved in Japanese business seem more interested in politics as a whole, though they find the whole business difficult to follow as it often seems to be based on nothing more than personality and petty infighting.

The impact of bureaucratic restructuring

In light of the above problems, there have been recent attempts to challenge the power of the Japanese bureaucracy. As a result of the scandals involving bureaucratic contact with industry officials, for example, officials are effectively prohibited from receiving entertainment or goods. I have even heard a case in which a cup of coffee at a café meeting was refused by a senior ministry official in the immediate aftermath of the scandals (a 1998 conversation with Democratic Party research staff member). Moreover, career bureaucrats are prohibited from taking up posts in industry for two years after leaving a government agency to limit the possible abuses caused by *amakudari*. In actual fact, however, *amakudari* continues all the same (see Table 7.1). Moreover, the pattern of former MOF officials remains unchanged as a large number continue to go to regional banks along with former Bank of Japan officials (*Asahi Shimbun*, 24 July 1999).

These special corporations are a particular focus of attention due

Table 7.1 *Amakudari* of former officials into special public corporations

Agency	Number of corporations	Number of former officials
Ministry of Finance	30	36
Ministry of International Trade and Industry	18	39
Ministry of Transport	15	31
Land Agency	15	18
Ministry of Construction	11	27
Ministry of Agriculture	11	27
Police Agency	10	10
Ministry of Health and Welfare	9	14
Ministry of Education	8	17
Home Ministry	8	9

Source: *Mainichi Shimbun*, 15 August 2000.

to the measures being implemented in the name of administrative reform. These organisations are meant to become more truly independent of the government, though judging from the continuing influx of former bureaucrats one might wonder at the extent to which this is possible. In any case, all the implications of the plans to cut their ties to government are unknown. In fact, it may not change much at all.

The main change to date is that the funds controlled by these corporations are no longer to be invested for public purposes. For example, government-controlled funds in the postal savings system, pension funds and other public controlled monies were used to buy equities in a bid to keep the Tokyo stock market from collapse in the period 1992–95. The cost to savers, future pensioners and others is unknown, but certainly losses were incurred and at best the rate of return was dismal. According to new guidelines, these funds can now be invested in higher return (and higher risk) portfolios. This gives the ultimate beneficiaries of these funds greater potential returns, but it also make the fund managers powerful institutional investors.

In addition to the new investment deregulation, the transfer of more of the special corporations to truly independent status should benefit the Japanese treasury. Many of the corporations still depend

The changing institutional structure

on subsidies or personnel from the government, and if these costs to the government are removed, real savings could be made. Since 1995, the number of such bodies has been reduced from ninety-two to seventy-eight, and more are to be abolished or merged. However, some public interest organisations will inevitably depend on the government subsidies, such as agencies for overseas assistance, tourism promotion and industry standards.

In addition to the changes in special corporations, there is some indication that administrative guidance is changing. Certainly there is anecdotal evidence that it is being challenged, though too much should not be read into individual stories. For example, there is the case of the publisher which publicly refused to accept administrative guidance. The company Kodansha, publishers of the weekly *Shukan Gendai*, were sent a letter from the Ministry of Health and Welfare in 1998 claiming that an advertisement in the magazine was in violation of the laws governing pharmaceuticals because it offers readers information on how to obtain prescription only viagra by postal order. The publisher took legal advice and continued with the advertisements (*Sankei Shimbun*, 16 July 1998). Admittedly, this may be less significant than it appears at first sight. After all, not all efforts at administrative guidance were successful even in the past. Moreover, administrative guidance is likely to be replaced with even more restrictions as informal powers are translated into clearly specified legal powers.

It is a fact that there has been a tendency for regulations to become more numerous as well as more specific despite talk of deregulation. One study (Tsuru, 1995: 115) found that in the period from 1988 to 1993, the number of activities which required government permission or authorisation actually increased despite efforts at deregulation in the period. Steven Vogel's study of deregulatory reform in Japan with extensive comparison with other industrial democracies is aptly titled *Freer Markets, More Rules* (Vogel, 1996). Even if the number of regulations were reduced, it is often the case that deregulation removes a burden of detailed intervention from a governmental agency but the streamlined regulatory framework permits new forms of even more effective, if selective, intervention. Deregulation does not necessarily mean a diminution in the powers of the bureaucracy.

This is true even if one accepts the clear trend of a reduction in the number and pay of central government civil servants. This reduction had already begun as a result of the administrative reform initiatives of the early 1980s. By 1994, the number had already been falling by

Table 7.2 Changes in Japanese central government structure and cabinet posts

Old ministerial portfolios	New ministerial portfolio
Ministry of General Affairs Ministry of Posts and Telecommunications	Ministry of General Affairs
Ministry of Justice	Ministry of Justice
Ministry of Foreign Affairs	Ministry of Foreign Affairs
Ministry of Finance	Ministry of the Treasury
Ministry of International Trade and Industry	Ministry of Economy and Industry
Ministry of Transport Ministry of Construction Land Agency Hokkaido Development Agency Okinawa Development Agency	Ministry of National Land and Transport
Ministry of Agriculture	Ministry of Agriculture, Forestry and Fisheries
Environment Agency	Ministry of the Environment
Ministry of Labour Ministry of Health and Welfare	Ministry of Labour and Welfare
Ministry of Education Science and Technology Agency	Ministry of Education, Science and Technology
Defence Agency	Defence Agency
Police Agency	National Public Safety Commission

1,300 persons per year to reach 859,212 (excluding military personnel). The numbers would have fallen further if not for increases due to a temporary expansion in state universities in the late 1980s and the new welfare and health services (*Yomiuri Shimbun*, 8 October 1994). All this is in keeping with current administrative reform initiative which is primarily aimed toward smaller government through streamlining. In theory, this should result in less cost to the taxpayer and a more dynamic, market-led economy.

The changing institutional structure

One of the major reforms occurred at the start of 2001 when the Japanese government reduced from twenty ministries and agencies to around twelve (see Table 7.2). For many of the ministries, the change is not so dramatic, but it is significant that the agencies transformed to the greatest extent are those related to the economy. The Posts and Telecommunication Ministry is effectively abolished and the remainder of its functions to be concentrated in a Postal Services Agency (temporarily located in the Ministry of General Affairs) to be privatised by 2006. The powerful economic ministries of Transport, Construction and Land are amalgamated into a super-ministry. Many other important functions are assumed by the Prime Minister's (PM's) Office, including the Finance Agency. In addition, the Economic Planning Agency is incorporated into the PM's Office to strengthen the policy making abilities of the prime minister and the cabinet.

Of course, there is no guarantee that the breaking up or amalgamating of agencies will have a desired impact. The Finance Agency is a point in case. The aim of the separation of the Finance Agency, responsible for the regulations of financial services, from the Ministry of Treasury, responsible for fiscal policy, was to weaken the overwhelming influence of the MOF and allow for better monitoring of financial services in the wake of financial scandals of recent years. Ironically, it was the MOF itself which proposed the creation of a Finance Agency even though the opponents of the agency have been calling for the break-up of the ministry for years. Moreover, one observer experienced in dealing with Finance Agency bureaucrats when they were MOF officials doubts the change will make much difference in any case (Okura, 1996: 186–7).

Rather than diminish the power of the bureaucracy, the new arrangements just mean a new pecking order. This suggests that the more important question is where will the powerful bureaucrats go? In the run-up to the separation of the MOF, the powerful bureaucrats opted for the Ministry of Treasury and shunned the Finance Agency. Clearly, certain agencies will still be important, some – such as the Ministry of Treasury or the Ministry of National Land and Transport – will become more so. Indeed, the current senior bureaucrats who have been successful in recent years are the ones who can protect bureaucratic interests in these difficult times.

A look at the senior posts of three of the powerful economic ministries provides an insight into the type of bureaucrat who can succeed in the midst of the turmoil. The last administrative vice-minister of the MOF, appointed in the wake of the June 2000 general election, was Toshiro Muto. He has a background in the Budget Bureau of the MOF during which time he was experienced in dealing with politicians over public works and construction project requests. His mentor was a senior MOF official who developed strong ties with the powerful LDP leader Shin Kanemaru, who died in 1993 just before he was set to be tried for kickbacks from the construction industry in exchange for public works projects (Irie, 1996: 37–8). Muto is said to be able to stand up to politicians as a result of this experience and used this ability to water down plans to reform the MOF (ibid.: 38–9). The result was that the new Ministry of Treasury retains all of the MOF's most important powers with the concession of the regulations of financial services transferred to the Finance Ministry. From well before his appointment, he was considered the most capable of defending MOF core interests.

However, if there was any doubt, the choice of administrative vice-minister is often a political football, one need only look at the selection of Muto's predecessor in 1999. The MOF administrative vice-ministerial post was the object of a bitter political struggle between the Kato faction of the LDP and the faction of the former Prime Minister Obuchi. Factions are the groupings which LDP politician use to promote their collective interests. There have been around five factions over the past few years, but the number varies with defections and attempts to split the factions by new leaders. Koichi Kato, a prominent figure in the LDP for the past decade finally succeed in creating his own faction in early 1999. While Kato had assisted Prime Minister Obuchi in gaining power, by 1999 Obuchi had formed a coalition with Kato's adversaries in other factions and the Liberal Party. In fact, the Liberal Party entered into a coalition government with the LDP in January 1999. Kato fought back by using one of his faction members, the Finance Minister, Kiichi Miyazawa, and was able to place his own candidate, Nobuaki Usui, as administrative vice-minister at the expense of the Obuchi faction candidate, Yoji Wakui. In these cases, the choice of personnel does matter. Kato's favourite, Usui, was a tax specialist known for implementing new taxes, including the controversial consumption tax and its subsequent increases. Wakai, on the other hand, worked to save the financial institutions under the Hashimoto government to the relief of the Obuchi faction of which Hashimoto was a senior member. It is not difficult to imagine the official advice that each would give in relations to further bail-outs or tax increases.

All this suggests that the reforms are likely to have an ambiguous impact. The bureaucracy will not be less powerful and the potential for scandal remains the same. The market will certainly play more of a role and government will be smaller, but remaining agencies will still be under the control of powerful bureaucrats. Politicians will continue to interfere, but with varying degrees of success. Only time will tell if they have protected or even extended the interests of their agencies, but the early prognosis is that little has changed. Certainly, senior bureaucrats are just as political as ever, and their political tendencies just as important to industry as ever.

Patterns of persistence despite administrative reform

The patterns of Japanese policy making did change temporarily under the various coalition governments which have been a key feature of the period after the fall of the LDP in 1993. Each of the coalition governments introduced new voices and complications into the policy-making process. Moreover, the coalition government have made various attempts to introduce encourage greater policy competence among MPs and reduce the powers and scope of the bureaucracy. However, not only has the dominant role of *zoku* MPs remained changed, it is actually reinforced by the reforms. To see how this happened, we have to look at the process by which these reforms have been introduced and the impact they have had.

While the LDP was out of power from 1993 to 1994, *zoku* MPs were largely absent from the policy-making process. However, this merely meant that the inexperienced ministers under the non-LDP coalition were even more dependent on bureaucratic advice and assistance. This had long been a problem even given *zoku* activities. Japanese Members of Parliament do not have an extensive staff in the same way as the members of the US Congress or even to the extent of British political parties. For many years, Japanese MPs only had two members of staff and both were occupied by constituency service. Members of Parliament were given the funds to hire an additional member of staff in the early 1990s who was to be a dedicated policy researcher, but actual implementation of the scheme has been patchy. The MPs have hired former colleagues who lost their seats or others who were not qualified to conduct policy research. Indeed, the training for such a qualification is problematic (*Yomiuri Shimbun*, 3 January 1997).

The temporary vacuum of MP power in 1993–94 led to the implementation of further changes in the policy-making capabilities of MPs. Ministers had been accustomed to using senior civil servants to respond directly to parliamentary questions. This has been phased out, however, so ministers must at least have some knowledge of policy to perform this aspect of their jobs. An even more far-reaching reform is the anticipated introduction of a new system of assistant-ministers (*fukudaijin*) who will possess power over subdivisions of a ministerial remit. The idea is to create a system much like the British system in which there are cabinet ministers and under them are ministers with specific areas of responsibility within the ministry. There is some similarity as well with the undersecretary posts in US government departments. These will be added to an expanded number of vice-ministers (*seimujikan*). Already the number of *seimujikan* has been expanded from one to two, and could go as high as four per ministry. The number of *fukudaijin* (minister for X in the British sense) will number between one to three per ministry.

In one sense, the creation of new posts compensates for the reduction in the number of cabinet portfolios from twenty to twelve to fourteen. Even before these changes, the realities of coalition government since the LDP returned to power in 1994 has meant that fewer coveted ministerial posts have been available because a few must go to coalition partners. These additional posts provide an alternative hierarchy through which an MP must rise before achieving a cabinet place. Indeed, a division of vice-ministerial posts into two has already occurred: the *sokatsu seimujikan* (general vice-minister) held by an MP with four or five terms in office, and the ordinary vice-minister post given to an MP with only two or three terms in office. Thus, an LDP career path has become more drawn out and complex.

There are problems with this proposed system which are relevant to business interests. The main dilemma is that the new system creates more entry points for influence by *zoku* MPs. In the past, ministers and even vice-ministers have been vulnerable to interest group pressures and even bribes, but the expanded number seems to invites more opportunities for scandal to arise (*Nihon Keizai Shimbun*, 19 April 1999; see also Kan, 1998: 162–3). This is likely especially to be the case if the occupants of the new posts do become more involved in administration as the reforms were intended to do. The former cabinet minister

The changing institutional structure

Naoto Kan envisioned the new sub-ministers and vice-ministers as part of a team chosen by the cabinet minister to form his or her own staff to run the ministry (Kan, 1998: 148). In the past, vice-ministers were chosen by the party leadership in attempt at factional balance, and Kan points out that when he was a minister he never even met his vice-minister once (ibid.: 160). However, there is no guarantee that the system will be used as Kan believes it should. In addition, these relatively inexperienced politicians are going to be met at every level by more experience career bureaucrats. In such circumstances, it is almost inevitable that the system will deteriorate to politicians seeking particularistic gain in exchange for bureaucratic assistance. That is, *zoku* politics will continue as usual but on an expanded scale.

These changes – along with the restructuring of ministries – have had an impact on other policy deliberation structures. The LDP PARC was transformed to reflect the new ministries and agencies, and parliamentary committee structures were also changed. The same is true with parliamentary committee structure. It is possible that bureaucratic reorganisation might even reinforce some patterns of *zoku* behaviour. Most intriguing is the new Ministry of National Land and Transport – predicted to control close to 80 per cent of the public works budget – which will be a magnet for *zoku* activities (*Asahi Shimbun*, 20 December 1999, evening edition). Similarly, the Ministry of General Affairs (MGA) will contain key regulatory agencies of keen interest to *zoku* MPs. In addition, the MGA will control the old Ministry of Posts and Telecommunication – a favourite *zoku* haunt – now reduced to non-cabinet agency status and soon to be privatised. Finally, the Ministry of Treasury will maintain the key budgetary and taxation powers of the old MOF and a focus for the interest of all MPs. Therefore, it is likely that *zoku* in some form will not only continue to play a role in policy making, but even see their influence concentrated in fewer and more powerful ministries.

As a final accounting of the current state of *zoku* prior to central goverment reorganisation, it may be useful to look at the MPs who can be identified as *zoku* MPs in 2000 as a baseline to assess any future change (see Table 7.3). First, there are consistent patterns of *zoku* activity across factions despite the fact that nearly all of the MPs first identified as *zoku* and factions to which they belonged have disappeared. The consistency of patterns in successor factions, with a few exceptions, indicates there is a pattern of recruitment and socialisation into specific policy domains. The only significant difference with

Table 7.3 *Zoku* MPs and factions (Lower House MPs only) in 2000

	Hashimoto	Kato	Yamazaki	Mori	Eto	Komoto	None
Commerce	24.1	17.2	24.1	17.2	13.8	0.0	3.5
Transport	26.3	31.6	15.8	0.0	21.1	0.0	5.3
Construction	28.6	35.7	3.8	14.3	10.7	7.1	0.0
Communications	25.0	15.0	15.0	10.0	20.0	5.0	10.0
iFinance	17.7	32.4	14.7	17.7	11.8	2.9	2.9

Note: Figures are in percentages and may not add to 100 per cent due to rounding.

previous lists composed in the 1980s is that *zoku* are more evenly spread across factions even though factions maintain certain strengths and weaknesses.

The bulk of this chapter has focused on the *zoku* with the clearest business interests. It needs to be emphasised that not all *zoku* are motivated purely by a symbiotic relationship with business interests. Those policy areas with minor business significance – welfare, labour, defence and education – often attract *zoku* with ideological or other concerns. However, even these ministries have economic implications and associated business interests. Even ideologically driven MPs are not likely to miss opportunities for assisting business interests through their specialised policy knowledge of a particular domain. Nonetheless, for this study I have chosen the five areas of *zoku* activity most relevant to business in order to demonstrate the continuity in the pattern of interest politics.

The patterns of the mid-1980s as revealed in Table 6.2 in the previous chapter generally still hold true. As the successor to the Tanaka faction, it is not surprising that Hashimoto leads a group which is strong across the board, but especially in construction. Moreover, following from Miyazawa's faction, Kato is strong in finance, though his faction is stronger in transport than before to an extent which challenges Hashimoto. The former faction of Nakasone split and resulted in two factions, the bulk in Yamazaki's and the remainder primarily in Eto's (also referred to as the Eto–Kamei faction). Still, the factions have become more evenly competent, or at least '*zoku* capable' over the past fifteen years, that is, with the exception of the Komoto faction and the MPs unaffiliated with any faction who just seem to survive somehow.

Therefore, the old 'rules' still apply though these are far from perfect in identifying *zoku* MPs. Any scheme must distinguish between those who temporarily occupy the post as a stepping stone and those who have chosen to specialise in a policy area. Moreover, senior politicians may occupy a number of key posts over their careers and so be identified in a number of areas as *zoku*. For example, Koichi Kato, whose position against rice import liberalisation started this book, was identified as an agricultural policy specialist (*zoku*) but he similarly has held senior posts in other areas which would indicate he was a *zoku* in those areas as well. In such cases, it seemed senseless to include senior figures who have a leadership role which requires experience in a number of potentially conflicting policy areas, though it is recognised that past experience and factional tendency might slant their approach to policy problems.

The exclusion of senior LDP leaders indicates another problem with any *zoku* identification scheme. Not all sources of *zoku* tendency are accurately captured by any scheme. In my statistics, I have only included those MPs who make a point of emphasising their policy domain experience in their profiles and have at least two of the requisite posts (with a leadership role in PARC or parliamentary committees, and as a political vice-minister). However, not all MPs with high *zoku* scores are necessarily likely to serve interest groups. For example, Junichiro Koizumi has held enough key positions to be identified as a posts and telecommunication *zoku*, but unusally for that group advocates the privatisation of the postal system. In addition, older schemes gave considerable weight to former officials of a given agency but I have found that many are better identified as *zoku* in areas outside their previous career. Nonetheless, I have included them and noted where they have an alternative focus.

The final important change is generational. Many of the top leaders of the LDP have retired, notably former Prime Minister, Takeshita. The remaining LDP MPs are much more vulnerable than before with key urban MPs such as Takashi Fukuya and Kaoru Yosano of Tokyo (both noted commerce *zoku*) in particular losing their seats in 2000. This rural bias cannot help but have an impact on LDP interest politics. Still, the party is always seeking to expand its links and new *zoku* MPs are starting to stake their claims. Indeed, if one looks at the most eager top two or three *zoku* in each faction across these five policy areas, it is apparent that relatively junior MPs are also prominent.

The finance domain may be changing as, following the creation of the Finance Agency, there is more of a distinction between the fiscal and financial services aspects of the old MOF remit, but nonetheless, this area is still dominated by the Miyazawa–Kato faction. In fact, Miyazawa's recent run in the ministerial post has only served to strengthen this connection even though he seems to be kept in place to reassure jittery financial markets. The Kato faction was the primary destination of former MOF officials, and had included up-and-coming *zoku*, such as Yoshitaka Murata and Fumio Kishida, the former himself a retired MOF bureaucrat. The split in the Kato faction after Kato's unsuccessful attempt to unseat Prime Minister Mori in November 2000, has left Kato's future in doubt, however. The bulk of the former bureaucrats in this faction split to form the Horiuchi faction in early 2001 and retain the predominant position as the top financial/ fiscal *zoku* faction.

The commerce and industry policy area is a key one for business but the content of its remit is complex. Still, many members focus on areas related to the needs of small business (though not exclusively). This area in particular is populated with younger MPs. Prominent among these are Ichiro Aizawa (five terms) and Yoshimi Watanabe (only two terms in office). It also contains former officials, including Tatsuo Sato (three terms) formerly of the Small Business Agency. I have not placed Kanbun Muto here because of his leadership role, but given his role in the party as a leading opponent of deregulation, I was very tempted to do so.

Transport and communication are the key areas of deregulatory reform and, perhaps as a result, the patterns of activity have become less clear with fewer members in each faction with less experience in relevant positions. Indeed, two of the most prominent positions are not only junior MPs but also from factions not normally associated with these policy domains. These are Tomoyoshi Watanabe (two terms – Yamazaki faction) in transport and Seiko Noda (three terms – Komoto faction) in communications. Nonetheless, the Hashimoto and Eto factions were involved in a bitter dispute over posts related to road construction in the summer of 2000 which indicates that the big players still view these posts as important (*Yomiuri Shimbun*, 16 July 2000). Moreover, both of the administrative vice-ministers for communications were from the Hashimoto faction as one might expect on past patterns.

The most controversial policy areas is, as always, construction. Just prior to the formation of the new cabinet in the summer of 2000, the former construction ministry Eiichi Nakao was arrested on bribery charges. Given that he was a member of the Eto faction, this faction withdrew its request for the ministerial post. The pattern of *zoku* influence, however, shows that the Hashimoto and Kato factions are the most active and, not surprisingly, the two vice-ministers chosen in 2000 included one from the Hashimoto faction and one from the Kato faction. In fact, the Hashimoto faction (through Obuchi, Takeshita and Tanaka) has reigned supreme in this area to the extent that one Hashimoto faction MP, Mamoru Nichida, has been called the *de facto* 'owner' of the policy domain (*Yomiuri Shimbun*, 2 July 2000).

The politics of old and new economies: public works and IT

There is no doubt that construction has been one of the most lucrative *zoku* domains and the connection with public works needs little explanation. If one adds to the picture the strong connection between public works construction and the Tanaka–Takeshita–Obuchi lineage, then the fact that under the Obuchi administration public works accelerated dramatically needs no explanation. It is a given that the extent of public works spending is a manifestation of *zoku* interest politics. This is unlikely to change despite recent moves to rethink public works spending. Indeed, such spending is only likely to be channelled into new areas to avoid the taint of the image of unneeded dams, harbours and flood control projects.

Japanese spending in this area is remarkable. Bank of Japan statistics comparing the level of public fixed investment as a percentage of gross domestic product (GDP) shows that Japan has the highest level among major advanced industrial counties (see Table 7.4). Moreover, this spending has been increasing in recent years in contrast to a decline elsewhere. This decline is particularly notable in the US and UK which have advanced the furthest in government deregulation.

There have been numerous attempts at justifying this spending. In fact, the Ministry of Construction website home page has a special section devoted to the defence of such spending. For much of the 1990s, the rationale for massive public works spending was that it was necessary to stimulate the economy and pull Japan out of its recession, and the alternative – tax cuts – would not work because Japanese have a strong propensity to save increased income rather than spend it in a way which would lead to economic growth (see, for example, *Far East Economic Review*, 11 March 1993: 13). A previous excuse used to be

Table 7.4 Public fixed investment/GDP (figures in %)

	1990	1997
Japan	6.6	7.8
USA	3.5	2.8
UK	3.2	1.6
Germany	2.3	1.9
France	3.3	2.8

Source: Bank of Japan, Kokusai Hikaku Tokei (International Comparative Statistics) as quoted in Kase, 1999: 19.

foreign pressure to stimulate the domestic economy and upgrade social infrastructure so that Japan would not be so export driven (Kase, 1999: 16). Prior to that excuse, there were the plans of Tanaka and his successors to restructure the Japanese archipelago for regional development. These are clearly excuses given that the more parsimonious explanation is the mutual gain for construction firms and LDP MPs as a result of such projects.

It is probably no coincidence that public works spending actually accelerated in the administration of Keizo Obuchi whose faction has been synonymous with construction *zoku*. Anyone who visited Japan in the late 1990s and visited the seashore or crossed a river could not help but notice the extensive public works activity. Figures indicating the scale of increased spending are difficult to identify because future spending is often being brought forward or deficit financing and burden sharing with local authorities is being used to fund the expansion. In the supplemental budget announced in June 1998, the increase in public works spending was the largest in history at 7 per cent (*Nihon Keizai Shimbun*, 23 June 1998).

The poltical impact of public works was demonstrated in the June 2000 general election when Yukio Hatoyama, leader of the opposition Democratic Party, tried to attack LDP reliance on such spending and the connection between the construction industry and the LDP. The attack was welcomed by many but supporters of public works in Hatoyama's own district were mobilised by the LDP to oppose him. This opposition was so strong that Hatoyama was forced to break off his scheduled campaign appearances to fly back to his district and address local concerns (*Yomiuri Shimbun*, 23 June 2000). The lesson for the politicians of all parties was clear.

The changing institutional structure

Ironically, the LDP itself had begun to question public works. In January 2000, the Construction Committee of LDP's PARC began to investigate ways to respond to the public criticism of the role of *zoku* MPs in public works planning (*Yomiuri Shimbun*, 21 January 2000). Not much progress was made until after the election, however. The Construction Ministry set up its own committe to re-evaluate its dams and river projects (*Yomiuri Shimbun*, 16 July 2000), and the Construction Minister, Chikage Ogi, effectively argued that no new dams would be built (*Yomiuri Shimbun*, 4 August 2000). The Chair of PARC, the senior LDP leader Shizuka Kamei, then embarked on an inspection tour of controversial projects in an attempt to show a sensitivity to the issue (*Yomiuri Shimbun*, 22 August 2000). At the same time, the LDP announced that it had established guidelines for a comprehensive review of public works spending (*Yomiuri Shimbun*, 23 August 2000).

These doubts about public works, however, need not change the importance of this spending for *zoku* MPs. For example, the announcement of the Mori administration that the main initiative of his second cabinet was promotion of the IT revolution meant that it was given centre stage in his announcement of a 3 trillion yen supplemental budget for 2000 including IT-related spending and public works spending (*Yomiuri Shimbun*, 16 August 2000). This will allow the LDP to respond to critics who argue public works money would be better spent on fibre optic networks and similar projects. Of course, this will mean fewer dams are built but this new economic infrastructure would still provide contracts to construction firms. Construction may be part of the old economy, but it can easily also survive in the new economy.

The IT initiative is a good example of a prime-ministerial agenda-setting initiative. It would be difficult to argue that it originates in Mori's interest in the subject; he had never even sent an e-mail until he did so during a photo opportunity after he became Prime Minister in April 2000. The question is, why did he chose this policy initiative? The easy answer is that IT is clearly a growth area intimately related to the future competitiveness of the Japanese economy. However, the motives might be more instrumental as well. After all, a popular new justification is needed for the LDP approach to policy. The old arguments in favour of roads, bridges and dams are no longer viable even in rural Japan, so a fresh and dynamic image as well as a shift in focus of public spending and policy was required. Moreover, the initiative can build on previous trial projects.

The problem with such an approach to public spending on infrastructure for the new economy has similar dangers to those of the bubble economy, even if it temporarily diverts attention from LDP scandal from the problems of the old economy. In fact, it creates the potential for more scandals. Politicians are not slow to exploit new opportunities and some are already using the Internet to raise funds (*Yomiuri Shimbun*, 25 February 2000). In addition, the cutting edge of the telecommunications industry has already produced its own scandal. When the opposition leader Hatoyama was accused of accepting illegal campaign contributions in February 2000, he not only denied the charges and filed a libel action against his accusers but also attacked the then Prime Minister, Obuchi, for receiving shares in the mobile telephone company, Docomo, though his personal secretary. While the receipt of the shares were defended by the LDP as an acceptable contribution as they were publicly listed, the ability of Obuchi and his administration fairly to deregulate the telecommunications industry was called into question. In any case, it is clear that this area of industry is no more immune from scandal than any other.

Indeed, despite the modern-sounding goals, the IT initiative is likely to continue the old interest politics. All the big electronics firms will want to get into the act, as well as the construction industry. Inevitably, policies aimed at building the IT infrastructure will also favour well-connected firms. This is classic *seisaku sho*. A preview of the potential waste can be seen in the numerous conference and concert facilities in the rural districts of LDP MPs – built at public expense with the latest electronic equipment – which are rarely used because there is no local demand for them. Recently a MITI official criticised this supply-led approach by suggesting that more emphasis should be put on demand-led investment (*Nihon Keizai Shimbun*, 31 August 2000). However, this would remove the opportunity for public works spending to the benefit of *zoku* clients. This is not to argue that the infrastructure is bad so much as to point out that *zoku*-driven spending is a burden on taxpayers and a waste of public funds. Even more significantly, it has a deleterious impact on the relationship between politicians and businesses in Japan as it creates a murky image of policy making. Moreover, the dangers to Japan given its political history and interest politics are obvious against the background of 'dot.com' bubbles and 'e-scams' around the globe.

Part III

The political organisation of business

8

The politics of Keidanren

In the previous two chapters we have seen how business has been involved in politics and enmeshed in the making of policy which shapes the business environment. However, the discussion leaves the impression of diffuse responsibility for dubious practices throughout the establishment and makes it difficult to pin the blame for structural corruption. Nonetheless, there are patterns to the type of business leaders who are empowered to become involved in politics. Normally, the most politically involved members of the firm are involved with politics as a function of their position in the business or business organisations. By identifying the patterns of selection for the key posts, one can identify the main politically active members of the business community. Thus, this chapter will not only reveal the pattern upon which leaders emerge but also assess the current leaders of the Japanese business establishment and provide guidelines for identifying future key players.

Collectively, business leadership is a self-replicating elite which seems to defy individual responsibility; the loci of responsibility can be found in business organisations. Moreover, the political tendencies of firms and organisations are shaped by these individuals who have a responsibility (often unrecognised) for the overall policy context, for bad and for good. This chapter looks specifically at the selection of national leadership in Japan's most powerful business association, Keidanren. If anyone is responsible for the role of business in Japanese politics, it is the type of individuals identified in this chapter together with the organisations and individuals identified as leaders in the two chapters which follow it. This is the political heart of Japanese business.

The origins of Keidanren

The most influential business organisation in Japan is without a doubt the Japan Federation of Economic Organisations. Its membership at the beginning of 2000 included 1,009 of the leading Japanese corporations (including sixty-three foriegn firms), as well as 119 industry associations. This is down from 1,013 firms and 121 industry-wide groups in February 1999. As membership in the association is restricted to firms with a large amount of turnover, the recession beginning in 1990 has eroded the membership slightly.

Keidanren was permitted by the Allied Occupation authorities which controlled Japan after defeat in 1945 to form as a successor to wartime business associations on 16 August 1946. However, they were compelled to respect the following guidelines (Nihon Keieishi Kenkyujo, 1978: 8):

1   Membership was to be voluntary.
2   No support was to be given to the *zaibatsu*.
3   Officials must be chosen by democratic procedures and the voice of small business in particular must be respected.
4   No officials could be under purge orders.

At its inception, Keidanren was a federation of the five major business associations: Japan Industrial Council, National Financial Associations Council, Japan Chamber of Commerce and Industry, Japan Trade Associations Council and the Central Council of Commerce and Industry Associations. These were considered primary members. Industry-specific associations were given secondary membership status with full membership rights. However, individuals and firms were only permitted to join as supporting members without voting rights. Public corporations and utility companies were also permitted membership.

With the end of the occupation, Keidanren was forced to reorganise. This was precipitated by criticism of Keidanren by the leader of the Japan Chamber of Commerce and Industry, Aiichiro Fujiyama, who argued that the Keidanren was too biased towards big business. In 1952, the Japan Chamber of Commerce and Industry and the Central Council of Commerce and Industry Associaions, both with predominantly small business membership, split from Keidanren. As a result, the remaining primary members merged and the organisation abolished the two classes of association membership. From this

The politics of Keidanren

point forward, the simple distinction was between industry associations and firms.

For most of the postwar period, the Keidanren has been unassailable as the main voice of big business in Japan. However, the association is also forced to speak with one voice. This means that it only takes a clear stand on those issues on which there is a clear common ground shared by all or most of the member firms and associations. This makes Keidanren conservative but it also gives it an important policy role. The leadership of the organisation, especially the chair, frequently comments on politics and policy, and it formulates proposals for policies and legislation. Keidanren officials often consult closely with the ruling party and the bureaucracy in the formulation of legislation, and Keidanren officials are usually key members of government special commissions set up to deal with difficult policy issues. Keidanren maintains over sixty standing committees covering major policy areas as well as issues of social importance to the firm, such as philanthropy and corporate governance, and Japan's bilateral economic relations with major countries and regions. These committees are chaired by the executive officers of major Japanese corporations and supported by the staff of the Keidanren Secretariat, called 'managers' or group leaders who number nearly sixty.

The organisation has also become conscious of the need for pro-business public information campaigns. During a visit to the UK in the late 1970s, Keidanren chair Toshio Doko was told by the Confederation of British Industry of how it needed a propaganda arm to combat the growing influence of the Labour Party in the postwar period, and upon his return to Japan, Doko ordered his staff to create an information service for Keidanren as well (Tamaki, 1997: 163–4). As Japan was experiencing a surge in support for the left in the 1970s, the need for such activities was manifestly clear and the Keizai Koho Centre, also known in English as the Japan Institute for Social and Economic Affairs, was formed in November 1978. The official English-language web page states that it was established 'in response to public criticism of business conditions following the first oil crisis and the subsequent five-year period of social confusion' – an interesting euphemism for the electoral success of the Japanese left in the late 1970s.

The leadership of the Keizai Koho Centre is similar to that of Keidanren as a whole and the chair of Keidanren is also the chair of the Centre. It issues publications and sponsors activities 'to create a favourable business environment within Japan and throughout the world'. The membership of the Centre is slightly larger than that of the Keidanren itself. Publications include an annual publication in English starting with *JAPAN 1980* which presents international comparisons of political, economic and social statistics and the *Kigyo Koho Kozo* (Enterprise Information Lectures) in five volumes in 1993. Its activites have ranged from a weekly television programme *Asu no Sekai to Nihon* (Tomorrow's World and Japan) and a variety of conferences involving business leaders and scholars, journalists, etc. as well as annual events such as the Enterprise Information Forum which continues to be held today.

More importantly, Keidanren played the central role in the organisation of political funds. While it never directly handled any money itself, individual members (both firms and associations) were assessed for political contributions which they then gave directly to the Liberal Democratic Party. In fact, it was one permanent official in the organisation, Nihachiro Hanamura, who was officially an 'adviser' to the organisation but was better know as the Business Political Bureau Chief of Keidanren during his long years of service as a political go-between. Keidanren suspended their activities as a coordinator of political funds in 1993, but agreed to continue their role until the loans taken to fund the LDP effort in the run up to the 1990 election were paid off. During an interview in the summer of 1999, the Keidanren official to whom I spoke was adamant that the organisation no longer played a role in funding.

As an alternative to direct involvement in political finance, Keidanren has made an attempt to encourage leading business figures to take an active interest in politics. They did this by sponsoring the creation of the *Kigyojin Seiji Forum* [Entrepreneur Political Forum] in July 1996. It has been most successful in bringing together corporate executives and politicians – primarily from the ruling LDP. Officials admitted that it has been less successful in encouraging corporate individuals to donate to political parties as an alternative to Keidanren-led funding. Keidanren also has its own internal committee on Business and Politics headed from 1996 to 1999 by Kenji Kawakatsu, Senior Adviser to Sanwa Bank, but the committee seems to have been relatively inactive. Since 2000 it has been led by Masahiko Furukawa, Senior Corporate Adviser to Mitsubishi Chemical, with the assistance of Matabe Maeda, chair of Maeda Corporation.

The politics of Keidanren

Table 8.1 Keidanren chairs (1948–present)

Name	Firm	Dates in office
Ichiro Ishikawa	Nissan Chemicals	3/48–2/56
Taizo Ishizaka	Daiichi Insurance, Toshiba	2/56–5/68
Kogoro Uemura	Bureaucracy, Keidanren	5/68–5/74
Toshio Doko	Ishikawajima HI, Toshiba	5/74–5/80
Yoshihiro Inayama	Japan Steel	5/80–5/86
Eishiro Saito	Japan Steel	5/86–5/90
Gaishi Hiraiwa	Tokyo Electric Power	5/90–5/94
Shoichiro Toyota	Toyota Automobiles	5/94–5/98
Takashi Imai	Japan Steel	5/98–present

Leadership selection in Keidanren

With the exception of refusing to play a part any longer in the channelling of political funds, the role of the Keidanren has changed little despite the political upheavals of the past few years. One area where this continuity, with perhaps gradual change, has been evident is in the type of officer selected to head the organisation (see Table 8.1). This is an important issue which deserves careful consideration. Its importance was clearly demonstrated during my interview with an official from the organisation who was very sensitive during my discussions on this subject. He flatly denied that there was any pattern or logic of selection despite considerable historical evidence to the contrary.

The first point to be made is that the government connection of most of the chairs is very strong. The first chair of the organisation, Ishikawa, worked for several chemical firms before he entered Nissan Chemicals in the early 1940s but he soon joined the Chemical Industry Control Board which was in charge of mobilisation of the industry for the military during the Second World War. Nissan was one of the new 'konzerns' which grew as a result of war demand in the 1930s and 1940s, but split up after the war. The second chair, Ishizaka, was a former Posts and Telecommunication Ministry bureaucrat, though early in his career he did quit and later participate in the management of Mitsui group firms. The third, Uemura, was a former bureaucrat from the Ministry of Commerce and Industry (one of the precursors to MITI), and in the powerful Cabinet Planning Board during the ascendancy of the Japanese military during the war. He was also the Keidanren officer in charge of relations with the political parties, including political donations, and was powerful even under Ishizaka. His assumption of the chair after Ishizaka was recognition of his key role. The remainder of the chairs, with the notable exceptions of Doko and Toyota, are from major firms with long histories of government ownership and/or control: Japan Steel (formerly Yawata Steel) and Tokyo Electric Power. Even Doko, with his experience at Ishikawajima Heavy Industries, and Toyota at his automobile firm, are drawn from heavy industry

The second noticeable feature is the relative absence of representatives of successor firms to the prewar *zaibatsu*, especially the big three: Mitsui, Mitsubishi and Sumitomo. While Allison (1986: 95) suggests that the former *zaibatsu* were represented first in 1974 as vice-chair of Keidanren, he is only referring to the prewar big three, and the late date of their presence is notable. This is especially true given that chair of the organisation are chosen from those who hold the post of vice-chair. The Mitsui group has done the best given the links it has with Toshiba and Toyota, but in both these cases, it is more that they are part of the postwar group by virtue of their relationship to the Mitsui main bank. These are not core Mitsui *zaibatsu* firms. Doko's longer career with Ishikawajima Heavy Industries places him close to the postwar Daiichi Kangyo Bank group as well. In any case, the Mitsui group came out of the war the weakest of the three major conglomerates and, perhaps, was not seen as a threat.

Some insight into the selection process can be gained by reference to a humorous article in the *Asahi Shimbun* on 8 May 1993 which gave predictions for the Keidanren chair 'Derby' for the 'Business Presidential Cup'. It handicapped fifteen potential contenders for the top post in Keidanren. The favourite of the commentators, including one member of the Upper House of parliament, was Sony's Akio Morita. The commentary pointed to his experience as a successful venture capitalist and his international experience and reputation. More seasoned observers, however, knew that this was not normally an advantage within Japan itself. In fact, the negative comments on most of the candidates was more enlightening than their positive political positions. The following types of firms were considered unlikely to win: former *zaibatsu* (Mitsubishi, Mitsui, Sumitomo), retail and distribution, food-related industries, trading companies. Keidanren staff put their money on Yutaka Saito, president of Japan Steel, a company

Table 8.2 'Hereditary' posts in Keidanren

Post	Prior occupant(s)	Occupant May 1990	Dominant firm
Chair	Yoshihiro Inayama	Eishiro Saito	Japan Steel
Vice-chairs	Eishiro Saito	Yutaka Takeda	Japan Steel
	Yutaka Takeda	Yutaka Saito	Japan Steel
	Eiji Toyota	Shoichiro Toyota	Toyota Auto.
	Masao Kanamori	Yotaro Iida	Mitsubishi HI
Committee chairs			
Chemicals	Shuju Hasegawa	Takeshi Hijikata	Sumitomo Cl
Defence	Gakuji Moriya	Masao Kanamori	Mitsubishi HI
Transport	Shojiro Kikuchi	Susumu Ono	NipponYusen
Distribution	Masayoshi Tozaki	Isamu Yonekura	Itochu Trading
Commerce	Tatsuo Minakami	Tadahiro Yatsuhiro	Mitsui Trading
Outer Space	Koji Kobayashi	Hisahiro Sekimoto	NEC

Source: *Asahi Shimbun*, 14 May 1990: 9.

which has frequently produced the chair. The *Asahi* itself opted for the chair of Toyoto Automobiles, Shoichiro Toyota, who did actually become the leader of the organisation. This constituted a shift from the past but this change must be put into perspective.

The early 1990s was an unusual period for Keidanren just as it was a dramatic period of political change in Japan as a whole. The first hints of political reform began to become an issue in 1990; the organisation of business was also being questioned. For example, Keidanren faced complaints over a lack of leadership and the stagnant nature of its leadership. The chair of Keidanren at the time, Eishiro Saito, was accused of lacking ideals and leadership and being more interested in golf and mah-jong. In addition, certain firms seemed to have monopolised posts in the organisation as Table 8.2 reveals, while industries such as retail, distribution and others were excluded (*Asahi Shimbun*, 14 May 1990).

Not surprisingly, the founder and president of the large retail chain Daiei, Isao Nakauchi, was among those critical of the business establishment, with Keidanren among the targets of his attack. He was clearly an anti-establishment figure who built his business fighting against major firms and the LDP. The major firms disliked him because his discount stores undercut their recommended manufacturer retail prices and the network of retail outlets they owned to sell their own goods exclusively to the public. The LDP disliked him because his supermarkets threatened small retailers which were the backbone of their constituency support organisations. Indeed, Daiei's success was one of the main reasons for the passage of the Large Retail Stores Law in the early 1970s which make further expansion by Daiei and others difficult. While Keidanren is perceived to be no friend of small business, it was equally unwilling to take on the political and economic establishment which prevented successful entrepreneurs from expanding their businesses.

Soon, however, things began to change. The first signs of change came with the appointment of Shoichiro Toyota as chair. While very conservative, Toyota and his firm have been no friends of the LDP. It is notable that the two 'outsiders' in the earlier discussion of Keidanren chairs, Doko and Toyota, were appointed in periods of serious allegations of political corruption with a significant business connection. Doko became chair at the end of the Tanaka administration and was outspoken in his criticism of the Prime Minister. Similarly, Toyota was chosen after the fall of the LDP and before the party returned to power in the summer of 1994. The outspoken criticism by automobile industry executives in the early 1990s and the ties of Toyota to the Democratic Socialist Party – a key party in the coalition government which replaced the LDP – were no doubt important factors in his selection.

It was also significant that Daiei's outspoken president, Nakauchi, was given a post as a Keidanren vice-chair in 1994. At the same time, Japan Steel seemed to be losing its previous dominance. It was argued by one source that this dominance arose from the fact that the steel industry was an important source of political funds and with the announced end of Keidanren's role as a political conduit, the industry has lost its place (*Asahi Shimbun*, 8 March 1994). It was significant that the industry with the largest group of vice-chairs in the new 1994 line-up was manufacturers of consumer electronics reflecting their continuing strength despite the faltering economy. Previous criticisms of Japan Steel's long-term dominance of the top post of chair was also a factor.

This reform movement was not sustained, however. By 1996, Japan Steel was trying to regain its position in the organisation against the newcomer Toshiba which had risen at the same time as the steel

The politics of Keidanren

Table 8.3 Keidanren leadership in March 2000

Name	Age	Firm	Post
Takeshi Imai	70	Japan Steel	chair
Yoshifumi Tsuji	72	Nissan Auto	vice-chair
Tsutomu Kanai	71	Hitachi	vice-chair
Katsunosuke Maeda	69	Toray	vice-chair
Toshifumi Suzuki	67	Ito-Yokado	vice-chair
Norio Oga	70	Sony	vice-chair
Satoru Kishi	69	Tokyo-Mitsubishi Bank	vice-chair
Hiroshi Araki	68	Tokyo Electric Power	vice-chair
Tetsuya Katada	68	Komatsu	vice-chair
Yoichi Morishita	65	Matsushita Electric	vice-chair
Minoru Makihara	70	Mitsubishi Trading	vice-chair
Akio Kozai	68	Sumitomo Chemicals	vice-chair
Shigeji Uejima	68	Mitsui Trading	vice-chair

Source: *Yomiuri Shimbun*, 9 March 2000.

firm lost its position of dominance. By 1998, Takashi Imai, chair of Japan Steel became the ninth chair of Keidanren and the company was back on top. Similarly, the addition of two new vice-chair posts in 2000 were given to the trading companies, Mitsubishi and Mitsui Trading, and though this was reported as an innovation – due to the need for their expertise in distribution networks presumably as such networks play a key role in the new economy – it was in reality merely restoring the position of trading companies at the top which they held ten years earlier. The only consolation was that the addition of new posts allowed the consumer electronics firms to keep their posts as well (see Table 8.3). Moreover, even though committee chair's positions are no longer dominated by particular firms as much as they were in the 1980s, unsurprisingly a similar type of top firm in each relevant industry still leads the major committees.

The 'rules' of leadership selection

In the absence of a major upheaval in Japan, it can be predicted that the same firms will continue to dominate Keidanren. The chair will likely be taken, as before, from among the vice-chairs. However, if this is the case, the future leadership candidates are in reality few. As with the choice of Imai in 1998, the contest will end up being between Japan Steel and Tokyo Electric. This seems to be based on the following rules:

1. There is a general avoidance of former *zaibatsu* firms. It will be interesting to see if this continues. If so, it would exclude nearly all the vice-chairs, but particularly the representatives from Mitsui Trading, Mitsubishi Trading and Sumitomo Chemicals.
2. Firms with potential financial difficulties are also unlikely to produce leaders. Therefore, given the continuing difficulties of the financial services sector, it is doubtful that a representative from Tokyo-Mitsubishi Bank will be made chair even ignoring the *zaibatsu* ties. One should note the demotion of representatives from Sakura and Sanwa Banks which were Toyota's vice-chairs, and Japan Life which was one of Imai's early vice-chairs. Nor will Daiei return to the leadership. It is facing serious problems – in 1999 it reportedly owed 2.6 trillion yen to banks and had posted a 25.8 billion yen loss in 1998 – which irreparably damaged Nakauchi's leadership prospects.
3. There are doubts whether Nissan's Tsuji can be a leadership prospect when the firm is now heavily controlled by Renault. Also, point 2 applies here: the debts of Nissan will be a problem.
4. There is the question of age. In 2000, Tsuji of Nissan was aged 72, and Kanai of Hitachi was 71 which put both older than Imai at 70. While the average age of Keidanren chairs and vice-chairs has fluctuated in the 1970s, there is an increasing recognition for the need for a younger business leadership.
5. There is also the question of industry. It is hard to imagine that Toray (a textile company) will be perceived as providing a strong leadership image. Even the representative from Ito-Yokado, which seems to replace Daiei as the large retailer representative, is not a top contender to represent all of Japanese business. The only interesting choice would be a representative of consumer electronics, such as Hitachi, Matsushita Electric or, more likely, Sony, to signal a change in the leadership of Japanese business.
6. International experience and orientation is still not seen as a positive attribute. This is part of the problem with the consumer electronics manufacturers, and why automobile manufacturers are unlikely despite the exception of Toyota. This will particularly

The politics of Keidanren 123

limit the potential candidacy of the Komatsu representative, with strong overseas interests, even though the firm has the right image (heavy machinery manufacturing).
7   The normal term for a Keidanren chair is being fixed at four years. By 2002, we will know if this has been maintained, or challenged by Japan Steel dominance.
8   A government connection seems essential. If so, the best bet is on Hiroshi Araki of Tokyo Electric Power, especially if the continued dominance of Japan Steel becomes an issue.

The lessons of these patterns in leadership selection suggest that the voice with which Japanese business speaks has changed little over the years. The same firms and industries tend to persist in the leadership for long periods, with change being painfully slow. A balance of a sort is maintained between firms and among industries, but the flux in vice-chairs merely allows two firms, Japan Steel and Tokyo Electric, to continue to dominate. Even at the level of committee chairs, there are only a small number of firms involved – around 50 or so – and the representatives of a handful of firms (Tokyo Electric Power, Sony, Komatsu, Itochu, Mitsubishi Chemicals, etc.) also chair key policy committees. It all means that similar interests and leaders with a set pattern of experiences will shape the official business position on politics and policy.

Conclusions

The focus of this chapter was on the Keidanren. This is natural given its predominant role as the main voice of business. Several issues have been raised with regard to the type of firm which gets involved in Keidanren and the impact that this may have on the policy advice represented to be the views of business. It is important to note that Keidanren is the establishment voice of big business while the Keizai Doyukai is more progressive and the Chambers of Commerce and Industry provides a more concrete service to small and medium-sized businesses. These issues will be explored in more detail in the next chapter.

9

Three other key national business organisations

While it was justifiable to use one chapter to concentrate on Keidanren given its importance in Japanese politics, it is not the only major business organisation in Japan. Indeed, the other top three groups play a crucial role in the business community. The Japan Chambers of Commerce and Industry is most notable for its close association with the state and the involvement of large numbers of small and medium-sized firms. The Keizai Doyukai is based on individual membership and plays a progressive role in the business politics. Finally, Nikkeiren, Japan's employer association, has historically been the voice of management in disputes with labour unions and the left.

Keidanren will not be dislodged as the main voice of Japanese business and, indeed, Nikkeiren may be absorbed into it. However, the other two play roles which Keidanren cannot fulfil. Keidanren sometimes criticises the outspoken Keizai Doyukai leadership but the ability of Doyukai leaders to speak freely allows fresh ideas into the business community and often pushes the conservative Keidanren along politically. Moreover, the Chambers of Commerce provides a service to the overwhelming majority of firms in Japan which the Keidanren with its bias toward large firms, often ignores. Indeed, the business community would be much more closed politically if not for alternatives to Keidanren.

Japan Chambers of Commerce and Industry

The Japan Chambers of Commerce and Industry is the oldest of the big four business groups. It was founded in 1878 just after Japan opened up to Western trade. The founder was Eiichi Shibusawa, one of the pioneers of modern Japanese industry, who aimed at fostering Japanese commerce and industry to avoid the domination of foreign economic powers. The organisation was from the start assisted by the government, though as Gerald Curtis points out, this was not unusual as most countries – including the US – saw some form of goverment encouragement of business organisation in this period (Curtis, 1975: 53–4). It was involved in prewar government policy initiatives, including attempts at industrial rationalisation, the formation of industry cooperatives and, during the 1940s, government control of resources and forced mergers of companies in order to mobilise the country efficiently for the war effort.

After the war, the special governmental status of the organisation was removed and it joined the other major business federations in the formation of Keidanren. However, after the Chambers of Commerce quit Keidanren in the early 1950s, its status was restablished by special law. It is unsurprising given this close relationship to the government, that the only two directors of the organisation (the *seimu riji* and *jomu riji*) are always filled by former MITI bureaucrats, by *amakudari*. This allows the organisation to play a very service-oriented role by explaining and coordinating the implementation of government policy.

As a whole, however, the Chambers of Commerce are very decentralised. The vice-chairs of the organisation are filled by the chairs of the regional branches of the organisation. In fact, the Chambers of Commerce is more truly national in character compared to Keidanren as the regional Chambers are virtually independent. The national chair is simply the head of the Tokyo branch and the national secretariat is housed in the Tokyo Chamber of Commerce and Industry building. It is also much more diverse than Keidanren because it has no restrictions on the size of the firm qualified for membership as with Keidanren. Even so, the organisation is dominated by the same type of major firms which control Keidanren. Only one small/medium-sized firm was represented among the thirteen member of the board of advisers (*tokubetsu komon*) who play a leadership role in the organisation and that was by the president of Matsuhisa, Kazuo Kamiya.

The policy role of the Chamber is similar to that of Keidanren – providing advice to the government and supplying the members of goverment commissions and advisory bodies – but it is more vocal in relation to policies which have an impact on smaller firms and more involvement in implementation. The Chamber of Commerce is the first stop for any business seeking advice and it provides a forum to discuss policy. The organisation's secretariat, run by the two former

MITI directors, contains various divisions, including at least three which are heavily involved in formation of policy: the small and medium business promotion bureau, the distribution bureau and the industry bureau (Chamber of Commerce interview). The leadership is also outspoken on contemporary politics. Immediately after the June 2000 general election, the head of the organisation – Kosaku Inaba – cast doubt on the election of the deceased Prime Minister Obuchi's daughter, Yuko, by arguing that simply because she is the daughter of the former Prime Minister, it is strange she should have been up for election. The comments were not directed only at this case, but the ever more frequent phenomena of hereditary MPs. Indeed, the bulk of the LDP is made up of such individuals but still he argued that they are no use in standing up to the major politicians who are an obstacle to a changing Japan (*Yomiuri Shimbun*, 29 June 2000).

One political aspect of the Chamber of Commerce which is less transparent is its role in political finance. The organisation runs an associated political finance arm, the Japan Commerce and Industry Alliance (*Nihon Shoko Renmei*), which almost exclusively funds LDP candidates. However, given that the Chamber of Commerce is in principle politically neutral, I was refused further information on the Alliance! The Chamber of Commerce has also had a tendency to work more closely on policy matters with the LDP since it has almost always been the ruling party, but the tendency towards coalition governments since 1993 has meant other parties have become involved as well. After the LDP formed a coalition with the Buddhist Party Komeito, Komeito MPs became more visible in the organisation. Moreover, the opposition Democratic Party is also beginning to make its presence felt more than the traditional left parties (socialist and communist) in the past.

As with Keidanren, there is a pattern to the selection of Chamber of Commerce officers. While it would not be useful to examine a list of all the chairs, which go back to the Meiji era in the late nineteenth century, the postwar leaders are important to note (see Table 9.1). The most important of these is Aiichiro Fujiyama. He was not only the leader of the organisation during the Second World War, but even after he was purged by the Allied Occupation, he returned to head the organisation once his purge order was lifted in the waning days of the Occupation in 1951. He then reasserted the independence of the Chamber and led it out from under the dominance of Keidanren. After retiring from the post of chair, he became an MP in

Other key national business organisations

Table 9.1 Postwar chairs of the Japan chamber of Commerce and Industry

Name	Firm	Dates in office
Aiichiro Fujiyama	Dai Nippon Seito (Sugar)	3/41–7/46 and 9/51–7/57
Ryutaro Takahashi	unknown	7/46–9/51
Tadashi Adachi	Oji Paper	7/57–9/70
Shigeo Nagano	Fuji Iron and Steel	9/70–5/84
Noboru Goto	Tokyo Kyuko	5/84–12/88
Rokuro Ishikawa	Kajima Construction	12/88–7/94
Kosaku Inaba	Ishikawajima-Harima HI	7/94–7/2000

the LDP and formed his own faction. However, he was never able to raise the funds to mount an effective challenge for the leadership of the party – despite running twice for the presidency of the LDP at great financial cost – because he did not have the backing of big business. This suggests the limits of the Chambers of Commerce. It is not so much that it does not have the resources to compete with Keidanren, it is more that it does not possess coherent political power to put one of its own in office. Even so, Fujiyama made the Chamber a much more visible and credible independent force by his actions in the early 1950s.

Fujiyama's successors have also been right at the heart of the business community even if less of a maverick than Fujiyama himself. Shigeo Nagano went from the informal influence he exercised as one of the four kings of business in the 1960s to the leadership of the Chamber. Similarly, Noboru Goto's term in office was relative brief but he was visibly active in politics beyond his official role. Goto's biggest error came when he stated the organisation favoured the introduction of a new tax but was forced to withdraw the statement under pressure from small and medium-sized businesses (Kato, 1994: 276–7). He was removed from his post a year later. Similarly, Rokuro Ishikawa's tenure in office was cut short by the construction scandals of 1993–94 when his company, Kajima Construction, was implicated and he was put under pressure to resign (including pressure from Keidanren officials). It has also been argued that he was vulnerable because he opposed new land taxes to prevent speculation and the end of political contributions by firms (*Aera*, 10 August 1993). In short, he was removed at the very time that the political reform movement was strongest in Japan and he seemed out of step with the times.

There is little to be said about Kosaku Inaba except that he has kept a low profile and maintained the smooth operation of the organisation. Inaba's tenure has gone so smoothly that he tried to stay in the post for a third term, but there was resistance from the other members who argued that the chair was limited to two terms. As a compromise, Inaba was permitted to stay in his post until July 2001 to see through an international conference held by the Japan Chamber of Commerce and Industry in the spring of 2001. His replacement as chair is Nobuo Yamaguchi of Asahi Kasei, a chemical firm which was heavily purged after the Second World War for its deep involvement with the wartime regime but has now diversified into a variety of areas including construction materials and pharmaceuticals. Yamaguchi assumed the chair at the relatively advanced age of 76 and was thus considered unlikely to hold the post for long.

Keizai Doyukai

The third major business federations is the Keizai Doyukai, also known in English as the Japan Committee for Economic Development even though it would be more accurately translated as the Association of Economic Friends. It was formed four months earlier than Keidanren, in April 1946, and has maintained an independent existence for the longest of any of Japan's postwar business associations. However, unlike the other associations composed of other organisations or firms as members, the focus of the Keizai Doyukai is firmly on individuals and, in keeping with this focus, has consistently reminded managers of their social and political responsibilities.

The Keizai Dokyukai was almost radical in the immediate postwar period. It advocated 'reform capitalism' which placed it closer to the early Democratic Party when it was formed in 1947 and the Japan Socialist Party which made a coalition with the Democrats from 1947 to 1948. Indeed, the organisation worked closely in support of the coalition. It favoured industrial democracy in firms and a cooperative relationship between management and labour. This is no doubt why the president of Keidanren at the time labelled the Keizai Doyukai as 'a stronghold of communism'. In fact, to the contrary, the Keizai Doyukai approach was left of centre but in alliance with the forces which sought to avoid the extremes of communism and prewar

Other key national business organisations

autocracy. When the conservative Liberal Party, closer to Keidanren, and the militant Japan Communist Party brought down the centre-left coalition and defeated the centrist parties in the 1949 general election, the policy influence of the Keizai Doyukai faded for some time.

It is still considered to be the most progressive of the Japanese business organisations. To a degree, the views can be seen as the product of differing economic interests. For example, the early firms most strongly represented in the organisation were those which would benefit from the promotion of heavy industry. Moreover, the ties of these firms to the old business establishment have been weaker. Finally, the initial membership was drawn from the young business professionals who gained as a result of the purge by the Occupation of the old *zaibatsu* business dominated establishment.

More recent policy initiatives by the Keizai Doyukai have been similarly progressive but more within the mainstream of the Japanese policy community. It is interesting to note that the Keizai Doyukai maintains an unusual governmental link: the chair or former chair of the organisation has also been chair of the semi-government think tank NIRA since the formation of the research institute in 1974. The NIRA was created under the Tanaka administration and many of its research priorities over the years have reflected Tanaka policies, and the director for many years was a former Tanaka adviser, Atsushi Shimokobe, former Director of the Land Agency. While nominally independent, most of NIRA's research staff are on secondment either from major firms or from major governmental agencies. In addition, the bulk of the firms are ones with former governmental links: Japan Airlines, Japan Rail, Tokyo Power, etc. The key posts are held by seconded or former officials from the Economic Planning Agency of the Japanese government. In fact, it is a favoured *amakudari* retirement destination for administrative vice-ministers from the Agency who have few options for such posts.

Even given this semi-govermental status, NIRA has a 'cutting edge' orientation in its research programme, though little of it is controversial. It was one of the first to promote serious discussion of corporate philanthropy and product liability, but it also has the dubious honour of supporting Tanaka's plans to redistribute central government agencies around Japan (with disastrous consequences for land prices) and former Prime Minister Takeshita's initiative which saw every local authority in Japan receive 100 million yen to spend as they chose (at the peak of the bubble economy). Nonetheless, it was also where the former Prime Minister Morihiro Hosokawa – leader of the coalition which ousted the LDP in 1993 – developed many of his policy ideas which still dominate the reform agenda in Japan.

The Keizai Doyukai attitude toward political contributions has also been very different from Keidanren and the Chamber of Commerce. It has always encouraged individual contributions to parties as part of the social responsibility of managers. Indeed, the officers of the organisation are prominent among the list of individual contributors to political parties, primarily the LDP. This approach has been copied by Keidanren after the it ended its sponsorship of corporate and industry association funding for the LDP.

The leadership of the Keizai Doyukai (see Table 9.2) is drawn largely from a similar pool of executives as the other two major business organisations, but there has been more of a dramatic shift over time in the top leadership. The first obvious pattern is a gradual shift from leadership by semi-governmental organisations to more completely private firms. Semi-governmental organisations and associations dominate the early years, as do the industries associated with economic reconstruction of the Japanese economy after the war. Another noticeable changes is the transition from short terms and multiple leaders to single leaders with more substantial terms of office. Not surprisingly, this transition occurred under the leadership of Kikawada who played a major role in focusing the organisation and giving it political influence. The official thirty-year history of the Keizai Doyukai singles out the Kikawada period as the most important in the organisation (Keizai Doyukai, 1976: 9–14). He recognised that the changing times required Japan to embrace openness to the international community and moved the organisation to a more positive attitude towards cooperation with the outside world. This stood in clear contrast to other business leaders who at the time were still trying to defend protectionism (see for example, Akimoto, 1968: 209–11).

Kikawada's successor, Tadashi Sasaki, was an MOF bureaucrat who had fought unsuccessfully against a business community initiative to allow a business leader to assume the presidency of the Bank of Japan. Sasaki resurrected some of the immediate postwar cooperation with labour at a time of increased union militancy in the 1970s, though this only attracted the right wing of the movement. The most political of the recent chairs has been Takeshi Ishihara who has been outspoken in favour of political reform even before it was popular to do so. His immediate two successors were not prominent and were

Other key national business organisations

Table 9.2 Leadership of the Keizai Doyukai (1946–present)

Name	Firm	Term
Kanichi Moroi	Chitsufu Cement	1946
Kei Hosoku	Japan Industrial Council	1946
Kohei Goji	Major Industries Council	1946
Banjo Otsuka	Japan Speciality Steel	1947
Shozo Hotta	Sumitomo Bank	1947
Koehi Goji	Major Industries Council	1947
Shigeo Nagano	Fuji Steel	1948–49
Shoshiro Kudo	Reconstruction Finance Fund	1948–49
Shoshiro Kudo	Reconstruction Finance Fund	1950
Shinsuke Asao	Nihon Yusen Shipping	1950
Shoshiro Kudo	Recontruction Finance Fund	1951
Aiichiro Fujiyama	Dai Nippon Seito (Sugar)	1951
Takeo Shoji	Asahi Electrical Industries	1952–54
Masamichi Yamagiwa	Japan Export-Import Bank	1952–54
Shoshiro Kudo	Recontruction Finance Fund	1955–56
Dozo Kishi	Japan Roads Public Corporation	1955–56
Dozo Kishi	Japan Roads Public Corporation	1957
Sohei Nakayama	Reconstruction Finance Fund	1957
Sohei Nakayama	Reconstruction Finance Fund	1958
Hideki Inoue	Japan Cement	1958
Hideki Inoue	Japan Cement	1959
Yoshizane Iwasa	Fuji Bank	1959
Yoshizane Iwasa	Fuji Bank	1960
Kazutaka Kikawada	Tokyo Electric Power	1960
Kazutaka Kikawada	Tokyo Electric Power	1961
Tatsuzo Mizukami	Mitsui Trading	1961
Tatsuzo Mizukami	Mitsui Trading	1962
Yoshiki Ninomoya	Toyo Soda Industries	1962
Kazutaka Kikawada	Tokyo Electric Power	1963–74
Tadashi Sasaki	Bank of Japan	1975–84
Takeshi Ishihara	Nissan Automobiles	1985–90
Masaru Hayami	Nissho Iwai Trading	1991–94
Haruo Ushio	Ushio Electronics	1995–99
Yotaro Kobayashi	Fuji Xerox	1999–present

short-lived. However, Yotaro Kobayashi promises to be one of the most important leaders in the organisations's history. He has a strong international standing and is prominent in the business community. Moreover, he has directly succeeded Ishihara in the NIRA link which suggests a strong policy interest as well.

Overall, the Keizai Doyukai has been ahead of Keidanren not only on policy but also in personnel. It is significant that Ishihara from Nissan was chosen as the leader of the Doyukai prior to Toyota, also from the automobile industry, being chosen as the leader of Keidanren. Moreover, the prominence of electronics firms presidents, Ushio and Kobayashi, as Doyukai leaders is a signal to Keidanren that the time is ripe for that industry to rise to the top of Keidanren as well. The fact that Kobayashi is from a firm with foreign ties sends an interesting message to the business establishment.

In 1999, the organisation also appointed its first female director, Harumi Sakamoto, vice-president of Seibu Department Stores; she was the first female officer of any national business organisation. Of course, the lack of such officers is reflective of the very small number of women executives. Professor Yuko Ogasawara of the Department of Sociology of Edogawa University in Tokyo notes that in 1996 women accounted for 43.8 per cent of women managers in the US and 27.0 per cent in Germany, but only 9.2 percent in Japan (Ogasawara, 2000: 15). Very few of these women reach the level in the firm at which they would be eligible for Keizai Doyukai membership, not to mention to be selected as leaders of Keidanren or the Chambers of Commerce. Nonetheless, another woman, Eiko Kono of Recruit, was added in 2000.

Overall, the Keizai Doyukai is the pace-setter for change in the business community. This is clear not only in the type of officers selected, but also in their approach to policy and politics. The leaders of the organisation may be less constrained than their counterparts in Keidanren. The Keizai Doyukai even conducted a campaign encouraging its members to come up with the most shocking policy proposals they could think of (*Nihon Keizai Shimbun*, 3 May 1999). This type of attitude is resented by other business organisations, particularly Keidanren. Keidanren spends its efforts in building a business community concensus on policy matters which the free speaking Keizai Doyukai leadership sometimes seems to undermine. However, this might also suggest a need for Keidanren to reform to make itself more flexible and dynamic.

Nikkeiren

The Japan Employers Association, *Nihon Keieisha Dantai Renmei* (Nikkeiren), is the fourth major business association in Japan. It has traditionally focused on employer–employee relations, and assisting firms with labour issues has meant that it is the least powerful of the organisations given its narrow remit. Given the transformation of the labour situation in the past decade, due both to the collapse of the Socialist left and the continuing economic downturn, the role and rationale for the organisation is in doubt.

Nikkeiren was the last of the big four business associations to form in postwar Japan. The Allied Occupation authorities were reluctant to allow an employers' association to form immediately after the war because they had yet to establish labour rights legislation which was a central part of their plan for the democratisation of Japan. The main laws protecting the rights of trade unions to organise were passed in 1947 and a Ministry of Labour was formed at the same time to monitor and maintain labour standards. It was only in the following year that Nikkeiren was permitted to form, though regional employer associations were given permission to operate earlier. By this time, a coalition government including the Japan Socialist Party backed by the major labour federations and a strong labour movement was clear evidence of the fact that organised labour was a force not to be denied in postwar Japan.

It is important not to associate Nikkeiren with the prewar business establishment which had been fiercely opposed to any recognition of the rights of workers to organise and had adopted a paternalistic approach. Nikkeiren was premised on an acceptance of organised labour and merely sought to give management the skills to understand and cope with their relationship, to the advantage of the firm. Nonetheless, Nikkeiren is broadly representative of the postwar business establishment. Therefore, it is closer in character and disposition to Keidanren than to the Keizai Doyukai, the latter of which seeks more positive cooperation from the labour movement.

Therefore, Nikkeiren policies are more consistently based on the interests of firms, but also by extension, the workers in those firms. It has been consistently opposed to the militant left, especially as represented by the Japan Socialist Party and Japanese Communist Party, but at the same time, is a staunch defender of the interests of workers. It has been more consistent than the other federations in advocating opening the Japanese market for agricultural products, though one might put this down to the desire to keep wages low through lower food costs. This is the reason for the open advocacy of agricultural imports in the face of LDP opposition noted at the beginning of this book. At the same time, Nikkeiren is using its voice in indirect support of the Japanese consumer. The same is true for its concern for the health and well-being of the Japanese workforce. It often supports the worker position in policy disputes over health care reform and pensions, so long as corporate interests are not too much affected. Thus, the organisation can be very progressive in some respects, while closed-minded in others. In the late 1990s, it established its own think tank and expanded the scope of its policy interventions, but it is yet to have the policy influence of the other associations. In fact, the openness of the debate at the beginning of this book is a sign of Nikkeiren weakness more than openness in the business community.

As a result, the future of Nikkeiren is in doubt. With the demise of the JSP and the diffusion of the political power of Japanese labour unions after 1993, its role seems unnecessary. Indeed, the main union federation in Japan, Rengo, has been frequently flirting with a closer relationship with the LDP. It was argued in the past that a merger of Nikkeiren with Keidanren was desirable, but it foundered on the strong loyalties officers and members have to an organisation once it establishes itself as an independent entity (Curtis, 1975: 63). The recent talks are also not a foregone conclusion. Unlike Keidanren, Nikkeiren has a national network of local branches which seem to be resisting being submerged into the more powerful Keidanren. The selection of Hiroshi Okuda as the new chair of Nikkeiren in 1999 seemed to doom the merger as he was on record as being opposed to the move, but in May 2000 a project team was formed to look at a merger at the national level only (*Mainichi Shimbun*, 18 May 2000). Even if the merger does not take place, Nikkeiren's influence will continue to be weak – unless there is a sudden upsurge in labour unrest.

Conclusions

The three business organisations examined in this chapter are very different in character and organisation but they all provide important diversity in the political representation of business in Japan. The Keizai Doyukai is the most outspoken and progressively oriented of the three, but the Chamber of Commerce represents a diverse and

Other key national business organisations

dynamic set of firms which also makes it seem more open than the closed-establishment image of Keidanren. Nikkeiren is also progressive in some ways, but it would not be surprising if it joined Keidanren. Only organisational pride maintains its independent existence. Even if it does merge with the Keidanren, a continued role for the other two organisations is not in doubt.

10

The politics of the organisation of industry

The previous chapter examined the four major business organisations in Japan operating at the national level. This chapter also looks at nation-wide organisations, but with a much narrower focus than the big four business groups. The first type of organisations to be considered are *keiretsu*, the economic conglomerates often believed to the successors to the prewar *zaibatsu*. *Keiretsu* often attract a disproportionate amount of attention in discussions of the role of business in Japan so it is essential to consider their political role at this point. The second set of groups to be considered are the industry associations which make up Keidanren which, after all, is a federation of industry associations as well as firms. The most outstanding feature of these organisations is their diversity, but it is possible to classify them according to the type and degree of their political involvements, as we shall see.

Keiretsu

Keiretsu, or corporate conglomerates, are often supposed to be at the centre of Japan's political economy, and it is the regular meetings of the presidents of the member companies which are the core of the alleged political power of the *keiretsu*. In reality, however, *keiretsu* are too diverse in history and composition to act as a coherent political force. It is true that there are some political tendencies and proclivities inherent within the *keiretsu* with the longest history, but the *keiretsu* continue to fade in importance as industrial restructuring continues.

This conclusion is not due to any preconceived notion. Initially, this area of the investigation was taken to be of central importance in the political organisation of Japanese business. Requests for interviews were focused on this aspect of Japanese business organisation and secondary sources were carefully analysed to tease out any indication that *keiretsu* played a role. Repeated assurances by informants that *keiretsu* ties were weakening were not taken at face value. Nonetheless, the lack of evidence of political involvement and pattern of ambivalence in current *keiretsu* ties clearly indicated that these were not important in a political sense though they may continue to have economic significance.

What are *keiretsu*? Under the Allied Occupation of Japan (1945–52), the Japanese were forced to dissolve the economic conglomerates (*zaibatsu*) which were believed to have contributed to the political conditions enabling the military to rise to prominence in prewar Japan. The *zaibatsu* were generally controlled by a family with a holding company at the centre of the group. The Occupation Authorities not only purged the top leadership of the main firms but also dissolved the holding companies. The confiscated shares were then put up for sale to the public to encourage individual ownership of the firms and a sort of economic democracy. However, the timing of the sale of the equities could not have been worse. They were made available at the same time as the Japanese economy was undergoing a serious downturn as a result of the fiscal austerity programme initiated by a US businessman, Joseph Dodge, who was sent to Japan in 1949 to deal with rampant postwar inflation. This meant that new investors to absorb the large amount of shares made available were nowhere to be found and so firms were encouraged by the government to buy shares to prevent a collapse in the stock market. Firms with similar prewar links were, of course, more confident in buying shares in the firms with which they had already been associated, and the main banks of the dissolved *zaibatsu* along with other financial institutions held a significant portion of shares in the firms to which they lent money. The family-run *zaibatsu* were dead, but they were replaced by main-bank centred interlocking economic groups or *keiretsu*.

Even if we accept the notion that the *zaibatsu* in some sense survived, only three of the postwar *keiretsu* can be traced directly to prewar *zaibatsu*: Mitsui, Mitsubishi and Sumitomo. The other *keiretsu* may contain elements of the other *zaibatsu* or economic concerns, but are centred on postwar main-bank relationships and draw together diverse elements of the prewar groups. The three most important of these are: Sanwa, Fuyo, and Daiichi Kangyo. Fuyo was itself a prewar *zaibatsu* but the postwar group includes elements of the old Yasuda *zaibatsu* and the Asano *zaibatsu*, while the more completely postwar Daiichi Kangyo Bank incorporates the remnants of the Nissan concern and the Furukawa group among others. Sanwa is centred mainly on firms in the Kansai area of Japan (Kyoto, Osaka, etc.).

Mitsubishi and Mitsui are still the strongest economic conglomerates in Japan. They both maintain public relations committees which emphasise the coherence and unity of the group ties. Yet, while their English language websites included a mention of a political role, the Japanese websites omitted this point and requests for interviews were denied on the basis that the public relations committees of the two groups played no political role. Instead, I was advised to contact the individual firms within each group. Of the two groups, Mitsui has generally been weakest in the postwar period. It incorporates the oldest layers of the Japanese elite, but its political conservatism is mostly manifest in its ties to the Republic of China in Taiwan where Mitsui had extensive prewar interests. This led them to maintain this link through the right-wing politicians Nobusuke Kiishi and Eisaku Sato, but it was continued in the 1970s and 1980s by the more ideologically ambivalent Shin Kanemaru. Mitsubishi has also been closely associated with the right of the LDP, also with Sato and in the 1980s with Yasuhiro Nakasone due in part to a strong shared interested in building Japan's military forces of which Mitsubishi Heavy Industries and other firms are predominant suppliers. Ironically, Mitsubishi also has strong ties to continental Asia, including the People's Republic of China, in contrast to Mitsui. Sumitomo similarly has heavy industry commitments but mining and raw materials give it a less political orientation.

The only general exception to the political neutrality of the *keiretsu* might be that they would be more reluctant to let their weakest members fail and so might oppose deregulation policies. The key point here is that *keiretsu* have both vertical and horizontal ties. That is, the horizontal nature of the *keiretsu* means that they cover a range of diverse firms across many areas of business from heavy industry to brewing beer. The main firms in the group tend to be concentrated in specific areas, but the groups include a number of peripheral firms which may not be competitive but are supported and nurtured by the group. The vertical aspect of the group comes from both suppliers and retail outlets, which similarly may not be competitive but are a source of intra-group *amakudari* and destinations for redundant personnel. Regulatory regimes that protect these less competitive firms may find support from the main firms. However, the primary arena of the *keiretsu* is the president associations (*shacho kai*) which meet regularly to discuss business of interest to the group. However, these meetings seem to play mainly a social role with some economic spin-offs in terms of increased trust and lower transaction costs. Even detailed studies of the function of these ties suggest that there is little evidence of direct political action as a result (Gerlach, 1992).

The best that one can say is that there is a sense of membership and identity created by interlocking ownership of equities in the firms and, even then, there is evidence of weakening ties. Given the intolerable burden of debt held by many firms, the equities at the centre of the *keiretsu* have been sold more openly than in the past, though admittedly the percentage of shares held by banks has not fallen appreciably with a decline from 41.4 per cent in 1989 to 35.5 per cent in 1997 (Otsuka, 1999: 4). More importantly, mergers between firms in different groups have helped to weaken *keiretsu* ties. This is particularly true with the banks at the centre of *keiretsu*. Daiichi Kangyo merged with Fuji Bank (Fuyo) and Kogyo Bank. Mitsui Bank merged with Tokai and Asahi Bank. The later of these was a major shock to the Mitsui group and the president of the bank at the time complained, when it was agreed to name the new bank, Sakura Bank, due to the loss of the Mitsui name (ECONO NAVI website, 1999: 1). More mergers across *keiretsu* lines are inevitable, and strategic alliances and cost-cutting by seeking less expensive parts and services will further weaken these ties. The interviewees who were willing to discuss the phenomena indicated that they saw *keiretsu* ties as increasingly less important but these were interviews with individuals from the postwar *keiretsu* with, presumably, less binding ties.

The conclusion is that even if we accept a continuing social role for the *keiretsu*, there is evidence that the political importance of *keiretsu* is weak or non-existent. One would have to resort to a highly suspect structuralist argument – arguing that the social and economic ties are sufficient to engender the political protection of an 'executive committee of the bourgeoisie' – in order to preserve a political link for the *keiretsu*. This type of hegemony of 'monopoly capitalism' is as difficult to disprove as it is to prove because it assumes unseen forces of capitalist development. The best that one can say is that there is no evidence that *keiretsu* are political agents in any sense.

Specific industry associations

Rather than *keiretsu*, the industry associations are far more important in Japanese politics. First, they are a key source of many of the leadership candidates for the main organisations discussed in the previous chapter. It is not unusual for leaders of the Keidanren to have previously been, or simultaneously to be, the chair of a major industry association. In a sense this is not surprising, since Keidanren is a federation of such associations even if firms can also be members and key leaders are identified primarily by their firm of origin. Industry associations are also important as the key actors in negotiations on specific areas of policy. They are the key contact points for both the bureaucracy and the *zoku* MPs, and associations may have key former bureaucrats or *zoku* MPs as senior officials, even chairs, of the organisation. However, it is important to divide industry associations into three types – establishment, political and policy coordinating – and to distinguish between major players in the industry and the associations of which they are a part (or which oppose them). This chapter concludes with an assessment of indications of change in 1999.

The establishment

The establishment industry associations are those industries' associations which have a strong relationship with the goverment by virtue of their close connection with the state. Examples are the Electric Power Association (*Denki Jigyo Rengokai*) as well as other utilities, and related industrial groups such as the Japan Gas Council (*Nihon Gasu Kyokai*) and the Petroleum Federation (*Sekiyu Renmei*). Steel has also been closely associated with the state. In the immediate postwar period it was one of the priority industries in receipt of subsidies and has maintained a strong relationship with the bureaucracy as well as generously supplying the LDP with political funding. The Japan Iron and Steel Federation is the main industry group and Japan Steel is the dominant firm (Lynn and McKeown, 1988: 26–8, 68).

The telecommunications industry also has a close relationship with the state. The main firms are the NTT 'family' of companies – Fujitsu, NEC, Hitachi and Oki – which have been exclusive suppliers to the telecommunications monopoly over the years. The NTT monopoly has been challenged in the late 1990s by three firms – DDI (a joint venture of Sony, Kyosera and others), Japan Telecom (a joint venture of Japan Railways, Sumitomo Mitsui and others) and Teleway Japan (owned by Toyota, Mitsubishi and the Highway Facilities Association). However, NTT dominance remains unaltered in large part because of a lack of progress in deregulating the market. Indeed,

DDI announced a merger with the international telephone service provider, KDD, and the mobile phone operator, IDO, at the end of 1999 in what was widely viewed as a desperate move to maintain the challenge against NTT (*Financial Times*, 17 December 1999). The industry associations in this area cannot be too involved in policy, given these divisions. NTT is also considered by Internet service providers, such as those in the Japan Internet Association, as possessing a favourable position protected by government regulation. In this area, associations are divided or opposed to the dominant firm but most of the main players are also part of the establishment.

The defence industry must also be considered to have a privileged position in relation to the state and is clearly part of the establishment. The main firms in the industry are Fuji Heavy Industry, Fujitsu, Hitachi, Ishikawajima Harima Heavy Industries, Kawasaki Heavy Industries, Mitsubishi Heavy Industries, Mitsubishi Electric, NEC and Toshiba. Most of these firms are well represented in Keidanren, and Keidanren's Defence Production Committee has played a major role in promoting their interests. The industry maintains a little known Defence Equipment Industry Association, but more important are the influential firms, especially Mitsubishi Heavy Industry, which act primarily through Keidanren. Active in the same area is the Japan Air and Space Industry Association.

The financial services industry associations used to be pillars of the establishment but the continuing crisis in the industry and scandals have considerably reduced their presence. The National Federation of Banking Associations (*Zenkoku Ginko Kyokai Rengokai*) was among the top contributors to the LDP prior to 1993, but in the years since the bail-out of financial institutions began, in 1997, it was thought wiser not to give any money to the LDP while its members receive public money. The Japan Securities Brokerage Association (*Nihon Shokengyo Kyokai*) used to be similarly close to the LDP industry but, while the LDP was out of power, the industry generously supplied the parties of the anti-LDP coalition with funds and so the LDP punished the industry by deregulating the industry and allowing banks to enter the brokerage business (*Foresight*, July 1994: 18).

The political

Some industries are more politicised that others and this is reflected in the nature of their industry associations. By politicised it is meant that they are heavily reliant on political involvement to protect and advance their interests. This often means close connections to the *zoku* MPs and LDP factions. The connections were made more obvious after the fall of the LDP in 1993 and its return to power the following year. This relationship will continue to be tested by pressure for regulation of the very industries which are the most heavily protected politically.

A good example of how political associations can be at the centre of political struggles is the Truckers Association. The chair of the All-Japan Truckers Association (*Zen Nihon Torakku Kyokai*) had been an LDP MP since its foundation in 1969. At the time of the fall of the LDP from power in 1993, the chair was MP Mutsuki Kato who happened to be one of the LDP MPs who had defected to a new party, the Japan Renewal Party. During the popular coalition government in which the Japan Renewal Party participated, the Trucker's Association had no problem with the fact that Kato was no longer with the LDP. However, in May 1994, when the longevity of the anti-LDP coalition government was in doubt, the association decided to elect the chair of the board of one of their member companies and removed Kato with the excuse that his assumption of the post of Agricultural Minister in the Hata cabinet meant he would be too busy for the position. The real reason, as one of the directors of the association was quoted as saying, was that 'if they had to present a petition to the LDP and their chair was from the Renewal Party, then the LDP might react badly' (*Yomiuri Shimbun*, 25 September 1994). If the Hata government fell, the LDP came back to power and their chair was an opposition MP, the possibility of retribution was a real.

Yet, the relationship had been rebuilt by 1998 when it was revealed that the Assocition had donated 22.5 million yen to forty-five LDP MPs on the eve of the party's decision in December to continue a 20 billion yen annual subsidy to the industry in the form of lower taxes on diesel fuel. The threat of removal of the tax break was raised by the then coalition partners of the LDP, the Social Democratic Party, which had favoured the move. The Association had no qualms about its action: 'You need to make donations when you ask for favours' Tokiro Asai, the chair of the Association was quoted as saying (*Asahi Daily News*, 29 October 1999). One can anticipate the contining need for the association to defend its interests in this way as one of the key reform demands in Japan is to introduce more competition in the haulage business to reduce transportation costs. The Association can be expected to fight such changes vigorously.

Politics of the organisation of industry

Another example is the construction industry owing to its close connections with public works. The industry was closely involved with the LDP, especially through its connection with construction *zoku* and the Tanaka and Takeshita factions. The *Zenekon* (General Federation of Construction Companies) scandal of 1993–94 damaged the industry but it remained a political force. As the LDP headed for an Upper House election in 1995, the industry supported the party with funding and personnel. Only in Iwate, the home prefecture of Ichiro Ozawa, leader of the largest opposition New Frontier Party at the time, did the local chapter of the association support the opposition, including supplying most of the key officers of the Ozawa's campaign committee (Kuji and Yokota, 1996: 23–57). Ozawa was a former Takeshita faction member and protégé of Shin Kanemaru. (Kanemaru ran the political construction racket for both Tanaka and Takeshita.) The construction industry needed to maintain access to the party in power, but by maintaining the link with Ozawa, the association had some insurance to gain access even in the unlikely event of the LDP losing power again.

The Construction Industry Political Association continues to be a generous donor to the LDP, though this has been criticised as a *de facto* kickback for massive spending on public works approved by the LDP under the Obuchi administration. There are signs, however, that the relationship may be changing. The reconsideration of public works is a direct attack on the industry, though this may simply be replaced by a new form of public works. More significantly, the LDP has already indicated that it will not bail out the firms in the industry that are heavily in debt due to the continuing repercussions of the collapse of the bubble economy (*Yomiuri Shimbun*, 16 July 2000). This is a contrast to the establishment banking industry which did receive a generous bail-out package.

Other industries have similarly been active politically in promotion of their interests. The pharmaceutical companies and the relevant pharmaceutical and medical supplies associations have been prominent in policy deliberations on changes to the pricing structure and funding for the national health insurance system in Japan. The increasing costs of a rapidly ageing population have meant that the government is eager to find ways to cut costs. Attempts to reduce costs at the expense of the pharmaceutical companies and the doctors who also profit from the current system are opposed by both the Japan Pharmaceutical Industry Association and the more powerful Japan

Medical Association which represents doctors. The main firms in the pharmaceutical industry are also well represented in Keidanren.

Not surprisingly, all the 'political' industries have been at the centre of attempts at deregulation. They have spent many years cultivating political support to avoid changes in the laws which favour them and it would be suicide for politicians to abandon them. The only difference between the political industries and the establishment industries is that the establishment industries are protected by virtue of their position at the heart of the establishment while the political industries must more openly purchase protection. The protection of these industries, establishment or political, undermines the core of the strategy for revitalising the Japanese economy, namely, the reduction of communication and transportation costs, and a reduction in public spending by controlling medical costs and reducing public works.

Policy coordination

A third key role of industries and associations is a policy-making and implementation role. This role has often been at the centre of the debate over the relative powers of the Japanese bureaucracy. From the point of view of the bureaucratic control advocates, industries seem to be led by officials into carrying out the bureaucracy's will. The advocates of the power of industry note that firms and associations only agree after negotiation with officials – often changing the policies in the process – and comply fully only when it is in their interests to do so (Samuels, 1987; Urui, 1996).

The types of behaviour covered in this category involve a degree of collusive behaviour by firms, usually through the good offices of the industrial association. This has been criticised by some as a violation of anti-monopoly politics through the sanctioning of official collusion (*kansei dango*)(Woodall, 1993). While some of these collusive agreements have been harmful to consumers or the taxpayer, the most prominent examples have been to deal with trade friction with the Japan's main trading partner, the US, or to manage the decline of non-competitive industrial sectors. Examples of trade-related collusion were voluntary export restraints on the export of automobiles in the 1980s and the requirement that a fixed percentage of foreign semiconductors should have a share of the Japanese market. Declining industries whose associations have been involved in collective action include textiles, shipbuilding and steel (Uriu, 1996).

Politics of the organisation of industry

Collusion is not so easy, however, when the industry is divided by conflicting interests among the member companies due to differences in such areas as size, competitiveness and in alliances with firms outside the association. It is often only when there is a lowest common denominator that the firms can agree to act in harmony to protect and promote interests in this way. The existence of official guidance and sanction makes the formation and maintenance of such agreements easier, but it cannot guarantee the continuation of agreement in the face of divergent interests or political pressure for change.

Change?

There are some indications that the situation is changing; some associations are less likely to be forced to become political and the political coherence of associations is declining. For example, one of the few associations willing to be interviewed, the Food Manufacturing Equipment Association, freely admitted involvement in a range of political activities in support of their members. However, since 1993, they have no longer been burdened with political contributions enforced by the Keidanren funding system. The individual interviewed expressed satisfaction that it was unnecessary for the association to make contributions to the LDP and it was a relief no longer to have to do so. The association was resigned to the fact that competition rather than collusion is an accepted priniciple for successful business. However, the association still lobbied MPs and participated in delegations to lobby MPs as necessary in furtherance of its interests (Food Manufacturing Equipment Association interview).

A similar change was announced by one of the most established of all industry associations, the National Federation of Banking Associations (*Zenkoku Ginko Kyokai Rengokai*) at a press conference by newly selected chair of the federation, Sugita, on 20 April 1999. Throughout the press conference, Sugita emphasised that the new role of the organisation was in the making of policy recommendations in relation to building a sound and health financial system. When Sugita was asked his views on the political role of federation, he replied:

> Political contributions are an issue for the judgement of each individual bank, but the Federation will not have anything to do with such contributions. This is only my view, but I think it is best if political contributions are made in the form of public subsidies and individual donations. This is the approach adopted in the revised

Political Funds Control Law and Party Subsidies Law, and overall I believe there is a trend toward the suppression (*yokusei*) of corporate political donations. However, at present the environment in which parties can rely entirely on public subsidies and individual donations does not exist, and until it does, it is inevitable that firms will want to provide support in accordance with the regulations of the Political Funds Control Law. As someone who knows the industry well, I will continue to have a relationship with MPs to give my opinion as necessary based on the state of industry. (website at zenginkyo.or.jp/newskaiken0420.htm (20 April 1999))

This seemed to constitute a real change in the organisation which only one year earlier had announced that its members had given 240 million yen to the LDP at the end of 1998. In the wake of the bail-out of the industry, the banks had promised not to provide political contributions so long as they were in receipt of public funds. These donations were justified as payments on loans made earlier to the LDP which had to be repaid. While individual banks, mainly regional banks, continued to contribute to the LDP, the peak industry organisation no longer was willing to play a coordinating role and some in the industry (as in others) took this opportunity to stop making contributions altogether.

Conclusions

It was important at the outset of this chapter to deal with the role of the *keiretsu*. It is also important to restate clearly here that the above discussion does not deny that *keiretsu* are a force in the Japanese economy nor does evidence of weakening ties mean the groups are no longer significant. However, it does insist that *keiretsu* plays no significant political role. That is, even if the vertical and horizontal ties of such groups are one of the obstacles to reform of the economy, the impact is indirect.

On the other hand, this chapter has not only reinforced the general academic view that industry associations are important but it has also made an important distinction between three types of associations. Scholars often choose one type or another as suits their arguments, but a discussion of business power must examine all three. Moreover, any association can be more or less of the three types at any given time. When legislation is pending in regard to an area of interest to the industry, the association can be political even when it is normally establishment in orientation. While the threat from the left was strong, all associations felt compelled to act politically even if this just meant providing their quota of political funds. Finally, the policy coordination role is more likely when an association needs the guidance of the bureaucracy to deal with a crisis or long-term problem in the industry. Yet, this process too can become political requiring funds to reinforce the loyalties of MPs.

The situation has been complicated by the changes in Japanese politics since 1993. While some industries and firms have felt less need to be political, the most political are driven to fight even harder. At the same time, some key industries are split between newcomers favouring change and the establishment favouring a more cautious approach. In this context, it is the major firms in the industry with establishment connections which seem to have the most influence. This leads us away from a focus on industry to an examination of the role and structure of the firm as a political actor.

11

Social factors and the political culture of the firm

Before examining the political role of the firm and its internal political dynamics, this chapter looks at some of the social factors which are alleged to have an impact on the business involvement in politics. In terms of social factors, it discusses regional and local influences as well as school and family ties. None of these are found to be of great significance but they cannot be ignored in any discussion of aspects of social organisation in Japan which may have political implications. Finally, the role of the great individual as significant as one might think.

It is the firm which ultimately must be the focus. Some firms in Japan are more political than others and this chapter explores the sources of political involvement. Once inside the firm, however, the structure of political responsibility becomes murky. This lack of transparency is a problem which seems related to the dubious connections that firms maintain with both organised crime and politicians. While there is an indication of attempts to change the lack of transparency of firms, the lack of recognition of the political nature of relationships is a serious obstacle to real progress.

Regional and local factors

There are fairly clear regional political tendencies in Japan which are a reflection of differing business interests as much as anything else. The northernmost Japanese island, Hokkaido, maintains a frontier spirit but the history of declining industries such as coal has shaped its politics. Historically economically deprived Tohoku (the Northeast) is still eager for development despite great advances in the postwar period. The Tokyo region tends to be dominant nationally. Tokaido (on the Pacific coast) is traditionally a vibrant industrial corridor. Kansai,

Social factors and the political culture

including Kyoto and Osaka, is the strongest business centre outside Tokyo. The smaller island of Shikoku also seeks development but still possesses natural resources in agriculture and fisheries which give it a distinct set of interests. Chubu, including Okayama and Hiroshima, are more industrial, as is Kyushu with the metropolitan areas of Fukuoka and Kita-Kyushu but, as with all regions, there is a vocal underdeveloped periphery.

In each of the regions investment decisions by business and government assistance schemes have had a political impact. The heavily urbanised areas such as Tokyo, Tokaido, Kansai, Chubu and Fukuoka tended historically to support the left opposition, putting workers at odds with the firms which supported the conservative LDP. Once migration to the cities from rural areas slowed in the 1960s, factories often were placed in rural areas where there were both greenfield sites and a ready supply of underemployed rural workers. In addition, regional development schemes – both national initiatives and schemes targeted at specific regions or localities – have encouraged firms to invest in less developed areas of Japan.

The political results have been that more and more manufacturing workers live and work in the established conservative political strongholds so dampening the effect of urbanisation and industrialisation on the decline in the LDP vote. In addition, local LDP MPs could take credit for regional development and business investments which improved the economic well-being of their constituencies. The fact that politicians take credit for investment and development is almost universal. Business respondents in interviews, however, were taken aback at the suggestion that their plant-siting decisions or investment decisions were political – the rationale given by firms is purely economic – but no one denied that it was impossible, just that they were unsure if it was conscious or not.

Some firms have always maintained local MPs beholden to them. This has not always meant only LDP MPs. Before 1993, one MP from Aichi prefecture was always elected from the Democratic Socialist Party with not only the support of the Toyota Automobile Workers Unions but also the encouragement of the management itself. In Hitachi, a Socialist MP was also regularly elected, though with less direct encouragement from the firm. Many of the MPs elected with the backing of Matsushita in the 1980s were based in the Kansai area where key factories are also located. Thus, even though the blatant attempts of firms to push forward candidates in the 1974 Upper

House election were unsuccessful, local MPs cannot help but be influenced by locally powerful firms.

There is only the most fleeting of evidence for continuation of this phenomenon since the introduction of a new electoral system in 1994. Under the old multi-member constituencies, an opposition party MP and an LDP MP could run and win in the same district since districts elected between three and six MPs and, therefore, the firm could support both. In fact, the LDP usually took two-thirds of the seats and the Socialists one-third in a typical district so the company could maintain links with the opposition, usually through the union, but the control of government by the pro-business LDP was also assured. Since the change to a single-member districting system, choices have become clearer. The evidence is merely circumstantial, but the fact is that the seats previously held by MPs clearly identified with major firms in their dominant localities have all but disappeared.

Indeed, major firms seem to avoid major politicians in their districts, and would have more success at approaching problems at a national level. A former manager of a top semiconductor manufacturer whose factory was in the district of a major politician confessed that he never had any interaction with the leader (Semiconductor Factory Head interview). His only direct political interaction was with minor or local politicians who sought to use their personal influence to secure favours for local clients, in costly but non-integral areas of operation such as procurement of office supplies. National-level politicians are so busy with leadership struggles and the day-to-day management of their affairs that they rarely have time to interfere. Successful firms are happy to avoid them. On the other hand, the Democratic Party leader Yukio Hatoyama has been criticised for not paying enough attention to the decline of the factory in his district, so less successful and minor firms may demand attention but are not likely to receive it merely due to local connections.

Evidence from a study of political contributions to politicians in the island of Shikoku (one of Japan's four main islands) found that significant contributions to local MPs were made by the president of a locally based firm with national economic activities (Kitahara, in Sasaki et al., 1999). One of the most remarkable cases was that of a consumer finance company president, Yoichi Kamiuchi of Promise, whose firm had grown dramatically as a result of deregulation of the financial services sector and anticipated more expansion as further regulations were removed. The need for political connections was

Social factors and the political culture

unmistakable (ibid.: 118). It may become more likely for locally based firms and executives to become directly involved in supporting local MPs as result of the new districting electoral system which makes the local party branch overlap with the constituency support organisation for the individual MP. Moreover, new funding rules requiring political donations by firms to be channelled through party branches will reinforce this tendency.

No study of regional factors in the organisation of Japanese business could ignore the traditional rivalry between the Kanto plain – greater Tokyo – and the Kansai region – including both Kyoto and Osaka. Osaka is one of the oldest commercial centres in Japan and was the main financial centre in the Tokugawa era as most local lords sent their rice to the Osaka market to have their rice stipends converted to money. The dominance of Tokyo as the new commercial and financial centre of Japan since the Meiji Restoration is strongly resented in Kansai. The problem is aggravated by the fact that Kansai continues to maintain its own vibrant business community. The main economic organisations all have major branches in Kansai but, despite their vitality, they seem to be secondary outposts. Even the staff of the Japan Chamber of Commerce and Industry acknowledged the resentment of the Kansai Chamber in particular owing to the fact that the head of the Tokyo Chamber is always automatically the national leader. Keidanren has frequently promised to work more closely on activities with its Kansai branch, but the issue persists. Even Kansai Keizei Doyukai behaves as though it is an independent organisation.

The problem cuts both ways. A firm may find its interests are best served by being a national player rather than wasting its energy on regional activities. One example was the case of Josei Ito, president of Nippon Life Insurance, who mainly resided in Tokyo due in large part to his activities as a vice-chair of Keidanren. He temporarily had his slot in the Kansai Keizai Doyukai filled by a vice-president of his firm but that vice-president died suddenly and the firm lost its senior position in the organisation. In 1996, the only member of the firm still active at a less prestigious level was another vice-president of the firm. This situation sent a clear message that the Kansai business community was secondary and was in stark contrast to the Akira Hirose, who had built up the business over thirty years and had only ever been active in the Kansai business community (*Foresight*, January 1996: 24). In some sense, the strategy of focusing on Tokyo makes sense once a firm is a success and, indeed, the major firms of Kansai are national players, including Sumitomo (including its extensive group of companies), Matsushita (which has a smaller but just as influential group of related companies) and the major trading firms of Itochu Trading, Marubeni and Nissho Iwai. Each of these groups and firms has representation at the highest level of national business organisation.

The list of powerful Kansai firms could also have included Kansai Electric Power and Japan Rail (JR) Western Japan (formerly part of the Japanese National Railway – JNR), but the power and rail companies are key regional players throughout Japan. In most regions of Japan, the electric power companies were politically prominent, not only in the regional business organisations but also traditionally in terms of political voice and political finance. Local rail companies had a much more political role in prewar Japan, but still are major political players, especially the new rail firms based on the old JNR. The remainder of regionally important firms are found in financial services, manufacturing and commerce, and vary by name and strength in each area but are politically and organisationally involved everywhere in local chapters of the Chamber of Commerce.

'Informal' and social sources of national leadership

Another key source of business influence can be said to be purely social. This ranges from the clubs in which both politicians and business leaders associate, to marriage alliances and old school connections. The impact of especially successful or prominent entrepreneurs is another possible source of political influence. Yet, the political significance of these factors is questionable, though no one should doubt that there may be isolated incidents or periods of time in which these factors might play a role. In general, it is more the formal organisation of business and the interests of specific industrial sectors or firms which provide the better insights into business and politics in Japan.

The most persuasive case for a political role for a social phenomena can be made in relation to the clubs, either exclusively for business leaders or open to business leaders, politicians and others. A number of such clubs and the links between business leaders and politicians have been emphasised by those looking at the relationship between business and politics (Roberts, 1973: 470–80; Yanaga, 1968: 56–62). However, Curtis has provided part of the answer as to why

Social factors and the political culture 153

they have declined in importance. He notes that Prime Minister Sato expanded the number of such clubs in order to reach a larger share of the business community and the role of clubs declined (Curtis, 1975: 48). With the proliferation of groups, the currency was cheapened and they became less influential. Coincidentally or not, the major business associations, particularly Keidanren and the Keizai Doyukai, became more organised and effective in representing business in exactly the same period. The political role of any remaining club is minimal.

At the same time as the clubs were in decline, there was also the demise of the 'four kings of business'. Yet, every generation laments the lack of key figures who can play a leadership role. All my interviewees insisted that the big names such as Morita, Ishihara, Matsushita and others were a thing of the past. Yet, studies of business political influence are continually filled with such names. For example, NEC's Hisahiro Sekimoto was used as an example of business community power in a textbook on Japanese business produced by Japan's main financial daily newspaper, *Nihon Keizai Shimbun* (Nihon Keizai Shimbun Sha, 1990: 195) It relates the story of how Sekimoto, while he was the leader of three electronics industry associations, joined with two younger company presidents – Fujitsu's Yamamoto and Fuji-Xerox's Kobayashi – to block a tax on office equipment. He took the time to visit the commerce *zoku* MPs one by one, listened to their views on the tax and then proceeded to block the distribution of political funds to the MPs who favoured the tax in exactly the amount that it cost the industry. In doing so, he succeeded in blocking the tax and achieved what five years of patient lobbying of MPs had failed to do. Yet, the lesson here is that although Sekimoto has slipped from prominence, Kobayashi has become head of the Keizai Doyukai, and this demonstrates that newer if lesser known leaders are produced all the time. They only seem impressive in retrospect.

It is true that sometimes it is the retired company presidents of the top firms in any given industry which have the prestige and distance to take bold steps or act as elder statespersons. They are the ones invited to sit on government commissions but even they will have some formal position in some private or semi-governmental organisation or business association. In fact, there are very few 'unconnected' individuals. Even entrepreneural success stories, such as Morita, Honda and Matsushita, who may be management gurus, have little of substance to say on politics despite their best-selling management books. Yet, all held top posts in Keidanren and so could not be considered complete mavericks. Thus, the idea that individual business leaders can be influential and politically independent of organised business must be dismissed.

The next source of potential influence is shared university connections. The leadership of corporations as well as the bureaucracy and political parties are drawn from a limited number of elite universities and departments within universities. In these institutions, graduates share experiences and rise in their careers at similar times. The University of Tokyo (*Todai*) is the most prestigious of these institutions and its graduates are sought after by the top firms. The *Todai* connection is also shared by the senior career bureaucrats at the highest levels of the Japanese government, particularly graduates of the Law Department. Other top state universities, primarily Kyoto, also produce a disproportionate share of top executives. Politicians on the other hand, tend to be graduates of slightly less prestigious private universities, such as Keio, Meiji and Waseda, but these too are represented among Japanese top executives. The Department of Politics and Economics at Waseda has produced a number of top politicians and they have maintained links with their alumni in a number of cases. One such case is that of Masanori Motoatsu, president of Itoen and adviser to the Japan Chamber of Commerce and Industry, who was selected by fellow Waseda graduate Prime Minister Obuchi to investigate ways in which his administration could assist small business in 1998 and 1999 as part of a major government initiative. This type of old school tie is not unusual elsewhere and it is doubtful if they are particularly significant.

Family ties between business leaders and politicians are the final social links to be considered here. These are the so-called *keibatsu* or blood ties which are supposed to have a deep social and political significance. These tend to be exaggerated by conspiracy theorists (see, for example, Hirose, 1997). It is true that business and political leaders intermarry their children in order to cement personal ties of trust and obligation. However, marriage alliances are notoriously unhelpful as even a cursory examination of the history of such alliances among European nobility would show. The marriages of the sons and daughters of business leaders and politicians are subject to less dramatic forms of stress than the wars and intrigues of Europe in the Middle Ages, but the results of such ties are just as fruitless. Moreover, the role of the executive wife in Japan limits the strength of family ties in any

Social factors and the political culture

case (Hamabata, 1990: 87–116). I could find no example of definite political consequences of such links.

Firm type and politics

In contrast to these social weak influences, the role of the firm is much more important. Obviously, the same political tendencies will apply to individual firms as to industry association, albeit with more subtle distinctions. After all, the membership of industry associations is comprised of individual firms. Nonetheless, the political proclivities of industry and firm can also be seen as distinct. Some firms consistently produce business leadership candidates and others none. This can be explained in large part due to what might be called firm political culture. Five sources of this political culture can be identified – position in the establishment, the political proclivities of the founder, corporate history, compelling interest to defend and hybrid types. However, two exceptions to these sources must also be noted: minimalism and lack of socialisation.

There is little doubt that a history of involvement of senior officials in the top business organisations creates an expectation of a knowledge of politics as part of the executive role. When I was a graduate student at Stanford, most of the Japanese students studying at the time for Masters degrees were 'executive track' (usually former Tokyo University graduates) who knew that politics was important for their future career. They were keen to talk about politics to get some understanding of the subject as part of their preparation for success. This was particularly true for firms which in hindsight were clearly part of the business establishment: Tokyo Electric Power, Japan Steel, Hitachi, etc.

The second source of political involvement is the fact that the founder of the firm played a big political role. Senior executives socialised under such an entrepreneur will feel compelled to maintain a presence to a degree, especially so long as the founder is still alive. Yet, this type of personal political proclivity can also have the reverse impact. I approached Matsushita Electronics for an interview and they strongly refused. Indeed, Matsushita industries seem to be trying to move out from the shadow cast by its illustrious founder (Matsushita correspondence; Okamura et al., 1994: 69–80). Matsushita's influence lives on, however, in the PHP Research Institute and Matsushita Training Institute. The latter of these has

Table 11.1 Matsushita Training Institute affiliated candidates (June 2000)

Name	District	Party	Won/Lost?
Tatsuya Kuroda	Saitama 11	Democratic	Lost
Hirokazu Matsuno	Chiba 3	LDP	Won
Yoshihiko Noda	Chiba 4	Democratic	Won
Hiroshi Nakada	Kanagawa 8	No Party Party	Won
Yasutomo Suzuki	Shizuoka 8	Democratic	Won
Koichiro Ichimura	Hyogo 6	Democratic	Lost
Shinya Ono	Ehime 3	LDP	Won
Satoshi Shima	Tokai PR	Democratic	Won
Kazunori Yamanoi	Kinki PR	Democratic	Won
Sanae Takaichi	Kinki PR	LDP	Won

been particularly active. It supplied one-quarter of the candidates for the Japan New Party which helped bring the LDP out of power in 1993, and it continues to be a key source of business-oriented candidates for the main political parties. In the June 2000 general election, for example, there were several successful candidates in both the LDP and the opposition Democratic Party who strongly identified themselves as Matsushita Training Institute candidates (see Table 11.1).

A third source of political culture is corporate history. This would include such firms as Nomura Securities which has a long and controversial history of political connections but continues to strive to maintain ties with both the bureaucracy and leading politicians. A fourth source is the imperatives of firms with specific interests to defend. This includes firms such as Mitsubishi Heavy Industries which has defence contracts and must take an active interest in defence policy, and construction firms such as Kajima Construction which is heavily involved in public works projects.

It must also be recognised that there are hybrid types. The private rail companies Seibu and Tokyu both had politically well-connected presidents who were part of the political establishment. In addition, their rail interests, and the retail outlets which developed as a result of their rail-related real estate holding, give these firms a complex political culture which could be taken by the current group of executives in several directions.

Social factors and the political culture

Of course, not all firms have a strong sense of political culture. In 1999, Toyota criticised Honda for refusing to assume the leadership of the Automobile Manufacturers Association. Honda argued that it is an active member but sees no benefit from assuming the burden of leadership and made the excuse that it is too small to fill the role. Honda also maintains a low-profile presence in Keidanren, but one wonders if it is just to protect its interests given the lack of enthusiasm for further substantial involvement. This is evidence that not all firms are eager for high-profile political involvement.

Another key exception to the political involvement of firms are the firms that are too small or not long established enough to qualify for leadership. Indeed, the fastest growing and the most profitable firms are also the least likely to have a prominent role in business associations. The exceptions are firms like Matsushita and Honda, which as we have seen, have been attempting to distance themselves from deep involvement. Indeed, most of the top 100 firms ranked by profitability and/or flexibility are nowhere to be seen in business organisations (Nikkei Best Firm Rankings, 1999 (see Nikkei website)). It is no surprise that newly established firms would be less likely to become involved.

Who is in charge of politics in the firm?

The issue of the political culture of the firm leads us to the internal dynamics of the firm to understand the sources of political leadership and involvement. In the firm, the role of the company president is paramount. This leads to a discussion of the recruitment of corporate leadership and the day-to-day management of the firm, both of which can have a profound influence on how political issues are dealt with by any company.

This discussion allows us to reach certain conclusions about corporate responsibility. In contrast to some authors who see Japan as a 'spiderless web,' company presidents must clearly take ultimate responsibility for the actions of their firms. This does not mean they must avoid politics but, equally, it does not mean that they can avoid responsibility for the political activities of their colleagues in the firm. By placing the company president at the political centre of the firm, an understanding of political behaviour, both inside and outside the firm, becomes much easier.

As noted above, there are a variety of factors which impinge on the political tendencies of the firm. The type of industry is the most important factor but size and a tradition of involvement are also important. Looking across the political history of Japan, however, it is difficult to find a sector untouched by scandal or at least with dubious links between the firm and politicians. Moreover, a firm without any political involvements seems rare, based on the evidence in the literature and notwithstanding the excuse given to refuse requests for interviews. Yet, the problem should not be political links – these should be expected – but instead we need to examine the lack of sources of accountability, internal and external.

The key image of Japanese firms held by foreigners is the single dedicated workforce, loyal to the company with an interchangeable leadership recruited through a plodding path to seniority. In contrast, the Japanese literature makes it clear that the company president is in charge (Nihon Keizai Shimbun Sha, 1990: 166–72). The board of directors are largely a rubber stamp for the decisions of the president. Even in the areas where the board seems to have nominal power, such as the election of their own membership, not only do presidents permit these elections as it provides valuable information on the factions within the firm, but they can ignore the elections if they choose to do so. Therefore, any political decisions, including those related to political contributions, are the authoritative decision of the president.

Factory heads (*kojocho*), bureau chiefs (*bucho*) and even section chiefs (*kacho*) under the bureau chiefs are most intriguing to other members of the firm and those interested in business, because they are visible role models of power and status to which the ambitious strive. Therefore, they are popular as characters in so-called 'salaryman' novels or *manga* comic books read feverishly by younger business readers. The generic scenario is one in which the ambitious bureau or section head is unsuspectingly mired in a world of corruption and politics. Sometime the hero survives and sometimes he becomes the scapegoat but the moral is always clear: it is a tough and dangerous world in which the weak and unwary will be used and discarded. In reality, however, this level of employee is not the political core of the firm.

The only exception to this rule is the bureau chief who heads the General Affairs Division (*somubu*) of the main corporate headquarters of the firm. The position of this post in the firm and the relationship of this position to the president makes it a political lightning rod. It was the General Affairs Division (GAD) bureau chief who was my

Social factors and the political culture

nemesis during my research in Japan, and it is his or her division which has the most to hide but is also the most important to defining the relationship between politics and the firm in Japan.

I discovered the role of the GAD bureau chief through a variety of sources and experiences. My experiences came first. A majority of my approaches for interviews were made via the Internet. Since websites are the responsibility of the Public Relations Departments located in the GAD bureau of Japanese firms, it seemed to be a natural choice for an approach. I did not expect much success in actually interviewing the top management of the company, but expected an interview with the public relations (PR) spokesman or woman from the firm. Yet, despite the use of the term 'PR' by Japanese firms, none seem to interpret their role as dealing with requests for interviews, either from academics or a potentially hostile press. Public relations in Japan means advertising and promoting the firm's goods and services. In retrospect, I can never remember having seen a Japanese corporate spokesperson speaking on behalf of a firm in crisis. Instead, one sees the press harassing reluctant company executives or, in their absence, company employees for comment in the absence of an official spokesperson.

Undaunted by the initial rejections, I still hoped to rely on several acquaintances and social connections. Once again, I was surprised that even this tactic produced no results. The universal explanation was that my initially enthusiastic interviewees suddenly backed out of the interviews after hearing from their superiors that it was not advisable. In all these cases, the rejection came directly or indirectly from the GAD bureau chief. My informants, who were still willing to speak informally, were not surprised when I indicated that requests through the PR section of other firms had been denied. They argued that the GAD bureau chief would have been the natural top of the chain of command for the PR sections so all requests had been effectively stifled at the same point.

It soon became clear that the GAD bureau chief in Japan is effectively the acting president of the company. He or she is responsible for the day-to-day management of the company along the lines laid down by the president. However, this situation leads to interpreting the role very conservatively. The expression 'not on my watch' amply conveys the sense that even though there may not be anything to hide, such an individual might naturally feel that it is better not to be too open just in case a problem does emerge. The fact that there may be questionable arrangements to hide, only reinforced their reluctance to speak.

The GAD bureau chief is responsible for finding the money for political contributions. This must be done in cooperation with the Finance Division Director but the GAD bureau chief retains authority for the transaction. However, GAD bureau chiefs are aware that this is not a normal operating expense. The finance director of one major firm suggested that GAD bureau chiefs may not want to talk because it is they who also have responsibility for dealing with requests for payoffs from organised crime specialising in the extortion of money from firms (*sokaiya*) under similar authority. The demand for payoffs from organised crime is a serious problem in Japanese business and all firms have a strategy for dealing with it. The implication was that it was a problem at the same level as dealing with the requests of politicians for support and, further, that there was a political dimension which might emerge in the context of interviews. It was surprising that the politics and organised crime were tied together in the minds of my informants, but the connection does exist.

Major Japanese politicians have had relationships with key figures in the criminal underworld (*yakusa*) in Japan. In fact, the example of the former Prime Minister, Takeshita, was raised earlier. A few LDP MPs have even been identified as gangsters themselves (Kaplan and Dubro, 1986: 110; Kurimoto, 1999: 168–72), and a considerably larger number have adopted the style and language of *yakuza*. Moreover, the right-wing movement in Japan maintains connections not only with LDP politicians but also with organised crime. Not all *yakuza* are politically right wing, but it has been an increasing tendency for organised crime to use a right-wing political organisational façade to approach corporations for payoffs.

This means that there is an ideological aspect to the problem of paying for protection. After all, why would major firms cave in to the demands of payoffs? While threats of physical violence, potential disruption to the business and even blackmail may explain some of the cases, there is also a sympathetic ideological dimension. Gangsters offer protection and the senior staff in some firms are not unsympathetic to the arguments of the criminals about the elements from which the firm needs protection, such as activists, critics, rivals and other gangs. This protection is couched in a language with which a segment of the Japanese business world could agree ideologically. This ideological sympathy helps explain the persistence of the

Social factors and the political culture

problem at particular firms. It also explains why the political protection afforded by Japanese politicians could be viewed as similar in character.

This brings us back to the political culture of the firm and the key role played by company presidents as responsible parties. Presidents choose their bureau chiefs and they also promote their successors to the board of directors and groom them. The consistent grip of certain firms on the leadership of business in Japan indicates the pattern of socialisation which has existed and continues to exist in Japan. Similarly, the persistence of scandal and relations with organised crime indicate a deep-rooted political culture of supporting this behaviour in the firm. Company presidents must take a large share of responsibility for cultivating and reproducing this culture.

Some changes have been proposed to deal with these problems and almost all have to do with increasing the transparency of activities within the firm. These include stricter outside auditing requirements which would make illegal payments more difficult to hide. There is also a move towards more open shareholder meetings and an increased awareness of the need for specialists in shareholder relations. Several major firms have created investor relations departments, mainly in reaction to a growing number of foreign investors in Japanese firms. Ironically, stockholder meetings originally became inaccessible as a result of the attempt of *sokaiya* gangsters to use them as a means to disrupt the firm in a bid to gain extortion money. However, this harmed the access of ordinary investors as well. Another major initiative is the addition of outside directors to the boards of major firms. While other business leaders often are recruited, there are a few academics and even foreign politicians, including former Philippine President, Curazon Aquino, and the British Conservative Party politician, Geoffrey Howe (*Yomiuri Shimbun*, 18 July 1999). All these changes will help but more will need to be done to transform the political culture of most firms, including the recognition that the problem needs to be confronted in the first place.

Conclusions

This chapter has examined a range of influences on the political tendencies of industries and firms. It has shown that the role of family ties and isolated individuals is not as important as often alleged, but regional factors can play a minor role. As noted in the previous chapters, the organisation of business is key to its articulation of interests and involvement in politics through 'normal' channels. Yet, within organisations it is the presidents of key firms who play the most important roles. Specific firms and industries have consistently been involved at the highest level of politics in Japan. Within the specific firms, then, we must look for the rise of political players. Ultimately, we must look to the president of the firm even if others play supporting roles. If anything is amiss, they must take responsibility. This holds at the national level as well.

12
Conclusion

This book ends where it began by re-examining the story related in the first chapter. The *Yomiuri Shimbun* newspaper editor worried about the murky world of business and politics in Japan but in the end it is obvious that he was both too optimistic and too pessimistic. He was optimistic because it had chosen two individuals who were at the periphery of Japanese politics at the time of their debate. Ken Nagano, at the time the leader of Japan's Employers Federation, *Nikkeiren*, was leading an organisation searching for justification of its existence and seriously considering merging with Keidanren. Liberal Democratic Party leader Koichi Kato was also on the outside of the Obuchi administration as he had opposed the coalition with the Liberal Party in 1999, and lost. Both the businessperson and the politician had reason to engage in public debate to stake a claim for a leadership role. As such, it was hardly a signal of new openness in the relationship between business and politics.

Yet, it would also be too pessimistic to dismiss the debate as unimportant. By identifying Kato as an agricultural policy expert, the newpaper was using a euphemism for *zoku* MP. While Kato is too experienced to be considered a simple agricultural *zoku* MP, he was playing their typical role of defending sectional interests against the general, in this case consumer, interest. Moreover, Nagano was expressing the deeply held belief of big business that regulations protecting political industries, including agriculture, had to be reconsidered for the sake of the rest of the economy. This was a clear clash of interests.

This debate is not so remarkable, however. Similar periods of open conflict were identified in the first two chapters of the book as it outlined the historical interests of business and how they are manifested in particular types of business players which can both conspire with and conflict with the interests of politicians. Yet, it was also shown in the three chapters on the policy-making process that it tends to emphasise the deep interpenetration of business and political interests which, in turn, tends to mask disagreements and creates a murky image of the relationship identified in the chapters. The disagreements between business and politicians have always been lurking in the background, but only appear in times of political scandal or economic crisis. Therefore, the underlying cleavages revealed by the debate between Nagano and Kato are not as unique as the writer suggests.

In order to unpack the complex of interests, this book has focused on the organisation of business from the national level down to the firm to reveal how business politics manifests itself. In doing so, it not only identifies the sources and range of interests manifested by business in the political process, it identifies the types of firms and posts with the heaviest burden of political responsibility within firms. By shedding light on these sources of business political involvement, it opens up the discussion of the nature of business involvement in politics in Japan. As a result, this final chapter uses this information to examine the problems of establishing a healthy relationship between firms and politicians in Japan.

Normative criteria for judging business involvement in politics

There are conflicting views on the nature of the relationship between politics and the firms which allow suggest conflicting options:

1. The liberal views the firm as a legal individual and as such it has responsibilities as a corporate citizen, including the need to play a positive role in the political system.
2. Radical critiques view firms as having a disproportionate influence over the political system and would discourage or heavily regulate business involvement.

These are paralleled by the main approaches taken in democracies with market economies to managing the relationship between business and politics: transparency and regulation. Both are present in the debate in Japan. For example, the movement towards the introduction of outside directors into firms is part of a transparency-led approach. The prohibition on direct corporate contributions to individual MPs is a regulatory approach. Thus, both views can be found in Japan. The

Conclusion

problem is that neither solution to the murkiness of the relationship is effectively pursued and enforced. Moreover, most firms in Japan seem to take a minimalist view of their role in politics.

The need for institutional and organisational change

This suggests that there must not only be more awareness that there is a problem but that a variety of solutions, both institutional and organisational, need to be addressed. These institutional issues include powers of the bureaucracy and, more crucially, the weakness of countervailing institutions such as the judiciary. The organisation of business also reinforces and perpetuates these institutional biases, particularly the bias towards large, established and parochial (non-international) firms in Keidanren. Yet, this also includes the reliance of business organisations on bureaucrats as well as politicians, and this applies to the Chamber of Commerce as well as the more politicised industry associations. While there is nothing wrong with a close relationship between the state and Japanese business, the neutrality of political decision making is seriously undermined when some groups have privileged access over others.

This may have been less of a problem when bureaucrats were involved but the rise of policy-competent politicians has caused the situation to worsen. The LDP and the other parties (which have become similar to the LDP in many respects) need to separate organisationally their policy-making and constituency-service functions. No doubt this is impossible to achieve completely, but simple changes – such as a 'members' register of interests', limitations on PARC committee members' time served, or standing down when the legislation involving major contributors is considered – could be very effective in making a first step. At the very least, there is a need for further research especially on the specific manifestations of the links between *zoku* and industry to monitor the situation.

Political contributions also continue to be a problem. The end of organised political contributions managed by Keidanren creates some problems as well as solves them. Instead of a centrally managed system of contributions, there is now more direct contact between the donor and recipient with more opportunity for problems to arise. Moreover, the move to channel contributions to constituency branches weakens the ability of the public to determine who gets what from whom. This would not be a problem if the branches of the parties were more centralised, and taking control of the branches could help, but given that individual MPs control local branches and these branches are now potential conduits for funding, problems will inevitably arise.

Another need is for more transparency. The government agencies responsible for monitoring political contributions make it very difficult to gain access to the information. A researcher is not allowed to photocopy the reports and only handwritten notes can be taken. This makes it difficult for scholars but, more importantly, makes it nearly impossible for citizen's groups to monitor conflicts of interest. The dispersal of political contributions through local branches controlled by a large number of local authorities will only increase fragmentation and make timely investigation of the reports more difficult.

Political leadership

This book has also demonstrated the important role that business organisation plays in the relationship between business and politics. There is a clear sense of corporate citizenship in Japan, but it is perhaps overdeveloped in some firms and lacking in many others. Organisational opportunities for more firms to become involved must be matched by an increased eagerness to do so from a wider segment of the business community than has been traditionally represented. The key business organisations, especially Kiedanren, need to restructure themselves to be more open to new firms and influences.

Admittedly, the ways in which interests emerge historically and obtain prominence is not based on conscious political goals. There has clearly been a pattern to the rise of business leadership and this is largely due to the historical trends, such as the transition from from light to heavy industry or government-associated to export-driven firms. It will be interesting to see if the rise of export-led firms and firms with strong links to foreign capital will finally have an impact on the top leadership of the key business organisations. As yet, the implications are uncertain.

Certainly, in each of the associations, with the notable exception of Nikkeiren, we have also seen how key leaders have raised the political profile of the association and given it a clear and more effective voice in public affairs. It has already been noted how Uemura enabled Keidanren to replace the loose social networks which had exercised business influence prior to his assumption of office. Similarly

Fujiyama re-established the independent existence of the Chambers of Commerce and allowed it to speak more clearly on behalf of small business in Japan. Kikawada maintained the Keizai Doyukai at the cutting edge of policy making but placed firmly it within the boundaries of the business establishment and gave it a more positive role. The question is, will the new leadership of Japanese business organisations similarly be able to manage business influence in a way which reduces the murky image of business political power?

Conclusion

While Japan's endemic corruption scandals are a cause for serious concern, Japan is not unique in these problems – only in their scale. Similar problems are experienced by other industrial democracies. At the same time, the blame should not be placed on aberrant individuals. The institutional and organisational structure of the involvements of firms in politics is the better explanation. These institutional and organisational issues must continued to be debated, and not just by politicians. Business must recognise the depth of the problem as well.

Bibliography

Newspapers

Asahi Daily News
Asahi Shimbun
Financial Times (London)
Mainichi Shimbun
Nihon Keizai Shimbun
Nikkan Gendai
Sankei Shimbun
The Nikkei Weekly
Yomiuri Shimbun

Magazines

Aera
Far East Economic Review
Foresight
Sentaku
Zaikai

Websites

Civil Watch – www.kiss-net.co.jp/civilwatch/amakudari
ECONO NAVI – www02.u-page.so-net.ne.jp/pb3/keiyu-t
Institute for Posts and Telecommunications Policy – www.iptp.go.jp
Japan Chamber of Commerce and Industry – www.jcci.or.jp
Keizai Doyukai – www.doyukai.or.jp
Keidanren – www.keidanren.or.jp
Ministry of Construction – www.moc.go.jp
Ministry of Finance – www.mof.go.jp
Ministry of Local Autonomy – www.mha.go.jp
National Institute for Research Advancement – www.nira.go.jp
Nikkei – www.neikkei. co.jp/report/prizm1.html
Nikkeiren – www.nikkeiren.or.jp

Bibliography

Books and articles

(Note: All Japanese sources were published in Tokyo unless otherwise indicated.)

Akimoto, Hideo. (1968), *Keidanren*, Sekka Sha.

Allison, G. (1987) 'Japan's Keidanren and its New Leadership', *Pacific Affairs*, 60:3, Fall, 385–407.

Asahi Shimbun Political Bureau (1994), *Renritsu Seiken Mawari Butai* [Coalition Government Behind the Scenes], Asahi Shimbun Sha.

Babb, James (1995), 'Japan's Ministry of Finance and the Politics of Complicity', *Review of International Political Economy*, 2:3, pp. 536–60.

Babb, James. (1996), 'The Origins and Nature of Japanese Electoral Reform' *Representation*, 33:4, pp. 151–61.

Blaker, Michael (ed.) (1976), *Japan at the Polls: The House of Councillors Election of 1974*, Washington, DC, American Enterprise Institute.

Calder, Kent. (1989), 'Elites in an Equalizing Role: Ex-bureaucrats as Coordinators and Intermediaries in the Japanese Government–Business Relationship', *Comparative Politics*, 21:4, pp. 379–403.

Calder, Kent. (1993), *Strategic Capitalism: Private Business and Public Purpose in Japanese Industrial Finance*, Princeton, NJ, Princeton University Press.

Curtis, Gerald. (1975), 'Big Business and Political Influence', in E. Vogel (ed.), *Modern Japanese Organisation and Decision-making*, Berkeley, CA, University of California Press.

Curtis, Gerald. (1988), *The Japanese Way of Politics*, New York, Columbia University Press.

Diamondo Sha (1980), *Jiji Mondai no Kiso Chishiki* (Basic Knowledge on Current Affairs), Diamondo Sha.

Dore, Ronald. (1999), 'Japan's Reform Debate: Patriotic Concern or Class Interest? Or Both?', *Journal of Japanese Studies*, 25:1, pp. 65–89.

Fujita, Hiroaki. (1980), *Nihon no Seiji to Kane* (Japanese Politics and Money), Soshobo.

Fujiyama, Aiichiro. (1976), *Seiji Waga Michi* (Politics My Way), Asahi Shimbun Sha.

Gerlach, Michael. (1992), *Alliance Capitalism: The Social Organisation of Japanese Business*, Berkeley, CA, University of California Press.

Hamabata, Matthews. (1990), *Crested Kimono: Power and Love in the Japanese Business Family*, Ithaca, NY, Cornell University Press.

Hanamura, Nihachiro. (1990), *Seizaikai Pipuyaku Hanseiki: Keidanren Gaishi* (My Life as a Conduit Between the Politics and the Business Community: An Unauthorised History of Keidanren), Tokyo Shimbun Shuppan Kyoku.

Hara, Yoshihisa. (1995), *Kishi Nobusuke – Kensei no Seijika* (Nobusuke Kishi – An Authorative Politician), Iwanami Shoten.

Heidenheimer, Arnold and Langdon, F. (1968), *Business Associations and the Financing of Political Parties: A Comparative Study of the Evolution of Practices in Germany, Norway and Japan*, The Hague, Martinus Nijhoff.

Hirose, Michisada. (1989), *Seiji to Kane* (Politics and Money), Iwanami Shoten.

Hirose, Takashi. (1997), *Shibutsu Kokka* (The Private Property State), Kobun Sha.

Holton, Robert. (1998), *Globalisation and the Nation-State*, London, Macmillian.

Hrebenar, Ronald. (1992), *The Japanese Party System*, 2nd edn, Boulder, CO, Westview Press.

Hunter, Floyd. (1953), *Community Power Structure: A Study of Decisionmakers*, Chapel Hill, NC, University of North Carolina Press.

Irie, H. (1996), 'Muto Toshiroga Shurei Dekinai Joken' (The Conditions Preventing the Emergence of Toshiro Muto), in K. Matsushita (ed.), *Kanryo Kyokuhi Jinji Roku* (Secret Bureaucratic Personnel Records), Takarashima Sha.
Itagaki, Hidenori. (1987), *Jiminto no Senkyo Himitsu* (The Secret of LDP Election Success), Sanichi Shobo.
Ito, Hirotoshi. (1996), *Hatoyama Ichizoku* [Hatoyama One Family], Pipuru Sha.
Iwai, Tomiaki and Inoguchi, Takeshi. (1987), *Zoku Giin no Kenkyu* (A Study of *Zoku* MPs), Nihon Keizai Shimbun Sha.
Iyasu, Tadashi. (1984), *Jiminto – Kono Fushigi na Seito* (The Liberal Democratic Party – That Strange Party), Kodansha.
Johnson, Chalmers. (1982), *MITI and the Japanese Miracle: The Growth of Industrial Policy, 1925–1975*, Stanford, CA, Stanford University Press.
Kan, Naoto. (1998), *Daijin* (Cabinet Minister), Iwanami Shoten.
Kaplan, David and Dubro, Alex. (1986), *Yakuza: An Explosive Account of Japan's Criminal Underworld*, New York, Macmilian.
Kase, Kazutoshi. (1999), 'Economic Aspects of Public Works in Japan', *Social Science Japan (Newsletter)*, 17 pp. 16–19.
Kato, Junko. (1994), *The Problem of Bureaucratic Rationality: Tax Politics in Japan*, Princeton, NJ, Princeton University Press.
Keizai, Doyukai. (1976), *Keizai Doyukai 30 Nen Shi* (The 30-Year History of the Keizai Doyukai), Keizai Doyukai.
Kobayashi, Shunji. (1976), *Kigyo no Seiji Kenkin: 'Moo hitotsu no toshi' no riron* (Corporate Political Contributions: The Logic of 'Another Form of Investment'), Nikkei Shinsho.
Kohno, M. (1997), *Japan's Postwar Party Politics*, Princeton, NJ, Princeton University Press.
Kubota, A. (1995), 'Big Business and Politics in Japan, 1993–95', in J. Purnendra and I. Takashi (eds.), *Japanese Politics Today: Beyond Karaoke Democracy?* London, Macmillan.
Kuji, Tsutomu and Yokota, Hajime. (1996), *Seiji ga Yugameru Kokyojigyo* (Public Works which Distort Politics), Enfu Shuppan.
Kurimoto, Shinichiro. (1999), *Jiminto no Kenkyu* (A Study of the LDP), Kappa Books.
Lynn, Leonard and McKeown, Timothy. (1988), *Organising Business: Trade Associations in America and Japan*, Washington, DC, American Enterprise Institute.
Mainichi Shimbun (Seiji to Keizai Bu) (eds.) (1991), *Zaikai to Seikai* (Business and Politics), Aipekku Puresu.
Mitchell, Richard. (1996), *Political Bribery in Japan*, Honolulu, University of Hawaii Press.
Morikawa, Hidemasa. (1992), *Zaibatsu: The Rise and Fall of Family Enterprise Groups in Japan*, Tokyo, University of Tokyo Press.
Muramatsu, Michio and Krauss, Ellis. (1987), 'The Conservative Party Line and the Development of Patterned Pluralism', in Yasuba Yasukichi and Yamamura Kozo (eds), *The Political Economy of Japan*, Stanford, CA, Stanford University Press, pp. 516–54.
Murobushi, Tetsuro (1981), *Oshoku no Kozo* (The Structure of Corruption), Iwanami Shoten.
Nakano, Koichi. (1998), 'Becoming a "Policy" Ministry: The Organisation and Amakudari of the Ministry of Posts and Telecommunications', *Journal of Japanese Studies*, 24:1, pp. 95–117.

Bibliography

Nakano, Minoru. (1997), *The Policy-Making Process in Contemporary Japan*, London, Macmillan.
Nihon Keieishi Kenkyujo (eds.) (1978), *Keizai Dantai Rengokai Sanjunen Shi* (The Thirty-Year History of the Federation of Economic Organisations), Keizai Dantai Rengokai.
Nihon Keizai Shimbun Sha (eds). (1990), *Gendai Kigyo Nyumon* (Introduction to the Contemporary Firm), Nihon Keizai Shimbun Sha.
Ogasawara, Yuko. (2000), 'Women Managers: Why Are There so Few in Japanese Companies?' *Social Science Japan (Newsletter)*, 18, p.15.
Okamura, H. Sasago, K., Sataka, M. et al. (1994) *Kigyo Tanken* (Investigating Firms), Shakai Shiso.
Okura, Kazutomo. (1996), *MOF Tan no Kokuhaku* (Confessions of an MOF Handler), Appuru Shuppan Sha.
Otsuka, A. (1999), 'Nihon no Kabushiki Shijo no Kozo Henka', at www.iptp.go.jp / research / monthly / mserch / finance / 1999 / no126127.htm (March 1999, pp. 1–25).
Pempel, T. J. (1998), *Regime Shift: Comparative Dynamic of the Japanese Political Economy*, Ithaca, NY, Cornell University Press.
Ramseyer, Mark and Rosenbluth, Frances. (1993), *Japan's Political Marketplace*, Cambridge, MA, Harvard University Press.
Ramseyer, M. and Rosenbluth, F. (1997) *Japan's Political Marketplace*, Cambridge, MA, Harvard University Press.
Roberts, John. (1973), *Mitsui: Three Centuries of Japanese Business*, New York, Weatherhill.
Saito, Bunmei. (1985), *Mitsubishi Soken no Kyoi* (The Threat of the Mitsubishi Research Institute), KK Best Book.
Samuels, Richard. (1987), *The Business of the Japanese State*, Ithaca, NY, Cornell University Press.
Sasaki, T., Yoshida, S., Taniguchi, M. and Yamamato, S. (1999), *Daigishi to Kane* (Members of Parliament and Money), Asahi Shimbun Sha.
Sato, Seisaburo and Matsuzaki, Tetsuhisa. (1986), *Jiminto Seiken* (LDP in Power), Chuo Koron Sha.
Schaede, Ulrike. (1995), 'The "Old Boy" Network and Government–Business Relationships in Japan', *Journal of Japanese Studies*, 21:2, pp. 293–317.
Schwartz, Frank. (1998), *Advice and Consent: The Politics of Consultation in Japan*, Cambridge, Cambridge University Press.
Shindo, M. (1990), *Gyosei Shido* (Administrative Evidence), Iwanami Shinsho.
Soderberg, Marie (ed.) (1996), *The Business of Japanese Foreign Aid: Five Case Studies from Asia*, London, Routledge.
Suzuki, Toichi. (1995), *Nagatacho Tairan 2* (Chaos in Nagatacho 2), Kodansha.
Tadamiya, Eitaro. (1963), *Showa no Seijikatachi* (Politicians of the Showa Era), Kobundo.
Tahara, Soichiro. (1986), *Sengo Zaikai Sengoku Shi: Sori o Ayatta Otokotachi* (The Warring States of the Postwar Business Community: The Men Who Manipulate Prime Ministers), Kodansha.
Taketsu, Fumio (ed.) (1992), *91 Gendai Seiji Joho* (1991 Contemporary Political Information), Guddotaimu Shuppan.
Tamaki, Kazuhiro. (1997), *Keidanren to Hanamura Nihachiro no Jidai* (Keidanren and the Nihachiro Hanamura Era), Shakai Shiso Sha.
Tsuru, Kotaro. (1995), *The Japanese Market Economy System: Its Strengths and*

Weaknesses, Tokyo, LTCB International Library Foundation.

Uriu, Robert. (1996), *Troubled Industries: Confronting Economic Change in Japan*, Ithaca, NY, Cornell University Press.

Usui, Chikako and Colignon, Richard (1995), 'Government Elites and *Amakudari* in Japan, 1963–1992', *Asian Survey*, 35:7, pp. 682–98.

Vogel, Steven. (1996), *Freer Markets, More Rules*, Ithaca, NY, Cornell University Press.

Vogel, Steven. (1999), 'Can Japan Disengage? Winners and Losers in Japan's Political Economy and the Ties that Bind Them', *Social Science Japan*, 2:1, pp. 3–21.

Weiss, Linda. (1998), *The Myth of the Powerless State: Governing the Economy in a Global Era*, Cambridge, Polity Press.

Wildes, H. (1948) 'Underground Politics in Postwar Japan', *American Political Science Review*, 42:6, December, 1149–62.

Wilson, Graham. (1985), *Business and Politics: A Comparative Introduction*, Chatham, NJ, Chatham House.

Wilson, G. (1990), *Business and Politics: A Comparative Introduction*, 2nd edn, Chatham, NJ, Chatham House.

Woodall, Brian. (1993), 'The Logic of Collusive Action: The Political Roots of Japan's *dango* System', *Comparative Politics*, 25:3, pp. 297–312.

Yamaguchi Hiroshi. (1983), *Jiminto Nidai Bunretsu* (The LDP's Great Split in Two), Tokuma Shoten.

Yamamura, Kozo. (1997), 'The Japanese Political Economy after the "Bubble": Plus Ça Change? *Journal of Japanese Studies*, 23:2, pp. 291–331.

Yanaga, Chitoshi. (1968), *Big Business in Japanese Politics*, New Haven, CT, Yale University Press.

Index

Abe, Fumio 51
Abe (Shintaro) faction 87
administrative guidance
   70–1
administrative reform 78–9, 82,
   93–4, 96–7, 99, 101–2
agricultural subsidies 5, 93
Aizawa, Ichiro 106
Allied Powers 23, 48, 114, 126, 133,
   137
All Japan Truckers Association
   [*Zen Nihon Torakku Kyokai*]
   46, 142
amakudari [descent from heaven]
   72, 74–5, 79, 86, 95, 125, 129,
   138
American Occupation 5, 126
   see also Allied Powers
Anzen Credit Bank 89
Arai, Shokei 53
Araki, Hiroshi 121, 123
Asahi 72
Asahi, Kasei 128
Asai, Tokiro 142
Ashida, Hitoshi 49
assen 62
Automobile Manufacturers
   Association 157

black market 23–4, 49
Bretton Woods system 6
   breakdown of 29–30
Britain *see* UK

bubble economy 3, 6–8, 12 ,44, 53,
   59, 63, 81, 83, 87–90, 110,
   129, 143
bureaucracy 7–8, 11, 23–6, 33, 45,
   62, 68–72, 76–8, 80, 85, 91,
   93, 95, 140, 147, 156, 165
   reorganisation of 45, 92, 94, 99,
      100, 103, 144, 154
   see also administrative reform
business organisations 8, 13
   influence on politics 3, 13–14,
      19–20, 27, 30, 70, 125, 127,
      148, 157, 162, 164, 166
   organised crime and 14, 160–1
   see also yakuza
   political contributions from 26,
      28–9, 33, 37–8, 41–2, 44, 47,
      50–2, 54, 56–8, 63, 126, 130,
      164–5
   see also political donations

cartels 4
   see also collusion
Central Council of Commerce
   and Industry Associations
   114
Chamber of Commerce *see* Japan
   Chambers of Commerce
   and industry
China 4, 23, 138
coal nationalisation scandal 49
collusion (*dango*) 144–5
constitution 39

corruption 2, 7–8, 11, 22, 30, 32–6, 40–1, 47–9, 51, 60–1, 63, 67, 71, 81, 91–5, 102, 106–7, 113, 120, 127, 143, 158, 161, 164, 167
Curtis, Gerald 2

Daiei 119–20, 122
Daiichi Insurance 117
Daiichi Kangyo 137, 139
DDI 141
decentralisation of industry 28
Defence Equipment Industry Association 141
democracy 48, 122, 133
Democratic Party (1948–55) 24–5, 49, 128
Democratic Party (1996–) 57, 90, 108, 126, 156
Democratic Socialist Party 6, 41, 120, 149
Denso 58
deregulation 2, 7–8, 30, 32, 39, 45–6, 63, 68, 73, 77, 97, 106, 110, 138, 140–1, 144, 150
Docomo 110
Dodge, Joseph 137
Doko, Toshio 29, 76, 115, 117–18, 120

economic crisis 3–4, 8, 44, 46, 63, 82, 107, 133, 137
economic recovery 2, 9
economic reform 9–11, 41, 45–6, 67, 86
Electric Power Association [*Denki Jihyo Rengotai*] 140
Eto–Kamei faction 61, 104, 106–7
extreme right 34–5, 160
 connection to politics 34
 see also yakuza
Ezoe, Hiromasa 33, 52

faction leaders 11, 27, 31, 50, 52–3, 60, 82, 84–5

factions 11–12, 42, 45, 52, 86, 100, 103–4, 106, 142
 fundraising by 31, 37, 56
 see also political donations
 weakening of 42–3
Food Manufacturing Equipment Association 145
France 7
Fuji Bank 131
Fuji Heavy Industries 54, 141
Fuji Steel 26, 127, 131
Fujita 21
Fujitsu 140–1, 153
Fuji Xerox 131, 153
Fujiyama, Aiichiro 27–8, 114, 126–7, 167
Fujiyama (Aiichiro) faction 27, 126–7
Fukuda, Takeo 28, 38, 52
Fukuya, Takashi 105
Furukawa, Masahiko 116
Fuyo 137, 139

GAD *see* General Affairs Division
gangsters *see* yakuza
GATT 4
General Affairs Division (GAD) 14, 158–60
Germany 7, 132
globalisation 3–4, 7
Goto, Noburo 127

Hachiman Steel 51
Hanamura, Nihachiro 116
Harbinger Party 55
Hasegawa, Shuju 119
Hashimoto, Ryutaro 42, 61, 98, 104
Hashimoto (Ryutaro) faction 106–7
Hatoyama, Yukio 59, 90, 108, 110, 150
heavy industry 20, 22–4, 26, 138, 166
Heisei Ishin no Kai (Reform of Heisei) 39

Index

Highway Facilities Association 140
Hijikata, Takeshi 119
Hiraiwa, Gaishi 40, 117
Hirose, Akira 151
Hitachi 29, 58, 122, 140–1, 149, 155
HIV scandal 92–3
Hokkaido, Takushoku 72
Holland 4
Holton, Robert 3
Honda 157
Hosokawa, Morihiro 130
housing loan corporation crisis 93
    see also Jusen

Idemitsu Petroleum 29
IDO 141
Igarashi, Mitsuo 78
Iida, Yotaro 119
Ikeda, Hayashi 25–6, 50
Imai, Takashi 117, 121
Inaba, Kosaku 126, 128
Inayama, Yoshiro 117, 119
industrial policy 8, 24
industry associations 13–14, 136, 139–41, 144, 146, 155, 165
    political funding and 140, 142–3, 145–7
insider trading 53
iron triangle 8, 68
Ishihara, Takeshi 37–9, 130–2, 153
Ishii, Susumu 34
Ishikawa, Ichiro 117
Ishikawa, Rokuro 127
Ishikawajima Harima Heavy Industries 117–18, 127, 141
Ishizaka, Taizo 117–18
IT (Information Technology) Revolution 82, 92, 109
Italy 7
Itochu Trading 119, 121, 123, 152
Itoen 154
Ito Josei 151
Itosei Trading 58
Ito-Yokado 121–2

Japan Air and Space Industry Association 141
Japan Chambers of Commerce and Industry 27, 53, 75, 114, 123–7, 130, 132, 135, 151–2, 154, 165, 167
    political finance and 126
    relation to government 125, 127
Japan Commerce and Industry Alliance [*Nihon Shoko Renmei*] 126
Japan Communist Party 129, 133
Japan Construction Industry Association Federation 57
Japan Development Bank 26, 73
Japanese Employers Association
    see Nikkeiren
Japan Fair Trade Commission 59
Japan Gas Council [*Nihon Gasu Kyokai*] 140
'Japan Inc.' 8
Japan Industrial Council 114
Japan Internet Association 141
Japan Iron and Steel Federation 58–9, 140
Japan Medical Association 142–3
Japan National Railway (JNR) 152
Japan New Party (1992–94) 41, 156
Japan Pharmaceutical Industry Association 143
Japan Rail (JR) 152
Japan Renewal Party (1993–94) 42, 78, 142
Japan Securities Brokerage Association [*Nihon Shokengyo Kyokai*] 141
Japan Socialist Party 25, 34, 38, 40–1, 49–50, 54, 128, 133–4
Japan Steel 29, 32, 118, 120–3, 140, 155
Japan Telecom 140
Japan Trade Associations Council 114
Johnson, Chalmers 9, 24, 69, 71

Jusen [Housing Loan Corporation] 44

Kaifu, Toshiki 52, 83
Kajima Construction 127, 156
Kajiyama, Seiroku 37, 45
Kamei, Masao 40
Kamei, Shizuka 78, 109
Kamiya, Kazuo 125
Kanai, Tsutomu 121–2
Kanamori, Masao 119
Kanemaru, Shin 34, 40–1, 100, 138, 143
Kan, Naoto 103
Kansai Electric Power 152
Katada, Tetsuya 121
Kato, Hiroshi 33
Kato, Koichi 1, 60, 100, 104–5, 163–4
Kato, Mutsuki 142
Kato (Koichi) faction 61, 100, 106–7
Kawakatsu, Kenji 116
Kawasaki Heavy Industries 141
Kawasaki Steel 29
KDD 141
keibatsu 154
Keidanren [Federation of Business Organisations] 27, 29, 37–43, 50, 57, 75, 113–21, 124–8, 130, 132–5, 140–1, 144, 151, 153–4, 157, 163, 165–6
   political funds and 42–3, 50, 57, 116, 118, 145, 165
   reform of 119, 132, 166
   weakening of 136, 139, 146
keiretsu (economic conglomerates) 5, 136–9, 146
Keizai Doyukai [Japan Committee for Economic Development] 39, 41, 75, 123–4, 128–30, 132–4, 151, 153, 167
   political contributions and 130

relation to government 39, 129, 132
see also business organisations
Keizai Koho Centre [Japan Institute for Social and Economic Affairs] 115
Kenzo, Uchida 40
Kigyojin Seiji Foramu [Entrepreneur Political Forum] 57
Kikawada, Kazutaka 130–1, 167
Kishi, Nobusuke 25–6, 50, 138
Kishida, Fumio 106
Kishi, Satoru 121
Kobayashi, Ataru 26
Kobayashi, Koji 119
Kobayashi, Yotaro 131–2, 153
Koizumi, Junichiro 105
Kokumin Seiji Kyokai [People's Political Association] 50
Komatsu 121, 123
Komeito 56–7, 62, 126
Kominto [Imperial People's Party] 34
Komoto, Toshio 52
Komoto (Toshio) faction 52, 86, 104, 106
Kono, Eiko 132
Kono, Ichiro 26
Kozai, Akio 121
Kumagai, Hiroshi 77–8
Kumano, Hideaki 78
Kyocera 140
Kyowa Credit Association 89
Kyowa Sugar incident 51

labour unions 5, 40, 133–4
   see also Rengo
land reform 5, 48–9
LDP *see* Liberal Democratic Party
Left 10, 30
   collapse of the 10, 133
Liberal Democratic Party (1955-) 8, 10–11, 26–30, 33–4, 37–41, 43, 45, 51, 57–8, 62, 68, 71,

Index

78, 84, 93, 109, 116, 119, 126, 134, 138, 140, 142, 150, 160
  dominance of 11, 50
  electoral decline of 30, 149
  fall of 36, 42, 44, 54, 101, 142, 156
  formation of 25
  promotion within the 84, 102
  see also seniority
  split of 42
liberalisation 6–7, 25, 39
Liberal Party (1945–55) 24–6, 49–50, 129
Liberal Party (1998-) 45, 56–8, 100, 163
light industry 20, 23–5, 166
Lockheed scandal 29, 51–2
low interest policy 6, 88

McKinsey & Co. Japan 39
Maeda, Katsunosuke 121
Maeda, Matabe 116
Maeda Corporation 116
Makihara, Minoru 121
Marubeni 152
Matsushita 30, 32, 58, 149, 152–3, 155–7
Matsushita, Konosuke 30, 149, 153, 155
Miki, Takeo 51
Minakami, Tatsuo 119
Ministry of Finance (MOF) 28, 69, 72–3, 75, 78, 81–2, 92, 94–5, 99, 100, 106
Ministry of International Trade and Industry (MITI) 9, 25, 69, 77–8
Minkan Seiji Rincho [Private Political Ethics Commission] *see Seiji Kaikaku Suishin Kyogikai*
Minseito 22
MITI *see* Ministry of International Trade and Industry

Mitsubishi 21–2, 29, 31–2, 48, 58, 60, 118, 121–2, 137–8, 156
Mitsubishi Research Institute 31
Mitsubishi-Tokyo 72, 121
Mitsui 21–2, 48, 58, 60, 118–19, 121–2, 137–9, 141
Mitsuzuka (Hiroshi) faction 60, 78
Miyazawa, Kiichi 82–3, 100, 106
Miyazawa (Kiichi) faction 60, 87, 104, 106
Mizuno, Naruo 26
Mizuno, Shigeo 26–7
MOF *see* Ministry of Finance
Mori, Yoshiro 59–61, 82
Morita, Akio 118, 153–4
Moriya, Gakuji 119
Motoatsu, Masanori 154
Muramatsu, M. and Krauss, E. 68
Murata, Yoshitaka 106
Muto, Kanbun 106
Muto, Toshiro 100

Nagano, Ken 1, 163–4
Nagano, Shigeo 127
Nagatacho politics 81, 83
Naito, Masahisa 77
Nakajima aircraft company 23
Nakajima, Yoshiro 54
Nakanishi, Keisuke 70
Nakano, Minoru 68, 81, 83
Nakao, Eiichi 107
Nakasone, Yasuhiro 34–5, 76, 82, 138
Nakasone (Yasuhiro) faction 60, 87, 104
Nakasone's Economic Policy Research Group 31
Nakauchi, Isao 119, 120, 122
National Federation of Banking Associations [*Zenkoku Ginko Kyokai Rengokai*] 141, 145–6

National Financial Associations Council 114
National Institute for Research Advancement (NIRA) 129, 132
NEC 58, 119, 140–1, 153
New Frontier Party 143
NGO see non-governmental organisations
Nichida, Mamoru 107
Nikkeiren [Japan Employers' Association] 1, 27, 40, 124, 133–5, 163
Nippon Life Insurance 151
Nippon Telephone and Telegraph (NTT) 32–3, 46, 76, 140–1
Nippon Yusen 119, 131
NIRA see National Institute for Research Advancement
Nishimatsu Construction 58–9
Nissan 8, 23, 37–9, 58–9, 117, 121–2, 137
Nissho Iwai 152
Nissho Securities 53
Nissin Textiles 26
Noda, Seiko 106
Nomura Securities 53, 156
non-governmental organisations (NGOs) 12
NTT see Nippon Telephone and Telegraph

Obayashi Construction 58
Obuchi, Keizo 23, 45, 61, 82, 88, 108, 110, 154
Obuchi (Keizo) faction 61, 100, 108
Oga, Norio 121
oil crisis 30, 75
Oji Paper 127
Okamitsu, Nobuhara 93
Oki 140
Okuda, Hiroshi 134
Okura 21
Omae, Kenichi 39
Ono, Susumu 119

opening of markets 1, 6, 30, 40, 134
  see also liberalisation
organised crime see yakuza
Osano, Kenji 24
Oshima, Ryumin 34
overseas development assistance 12
Ozawa, Ichiro 34, 37–8, 45, 53, 77–8, 143

PARC see Policy Affairs Research Council
Petroleum Federation [Sekiyu Renmei] 59, 140
Policy Affairs Research Council (PARC) 84, 103, 105, 109, 165
policy making 11–12, 67–8, 70, 76, 82, 101–2, 164
policy tribes see zoku
political donations 43, 47, 54, 58, 165–6
  to factions 43, 56, 60–1
  to individuals 43, 54–7, 60, 63, 145
  to parties 43, 54–5, 57, 59, 140–1, 143, 145, 165
political funding 28–9, 33, 37, 42–4, 49, 80, 84
  see also political parties
Political Funds and Control Laws see Public Election and Political Funds and Control Laws
political parties 48–9, 54, 165
  funding of 24, 27–8, 42–3, 57, 116
political reform 22, 38, 40–1, 43, 54, 83, 128, 130
  legislation 40, 43
prewar parties 22–3
protection of markets 4–6, 25
  agriculture 5, 31, 40
  retail industry 31, 40
Public Election and Political

Index

Funds and Control Laws 40, 49–50, 52, 54, 60, 62, 146, 151
Public Employees Association 40
public works 46, 63, 87, 107–9, 143
purge 129, 137

Ramseyer, M. and Rosenbluth, F. 68–70
rearmament 25
Recruit Corporation 32–3, 132
Recruit scandal 33–4, 36, 41, 52, 60, 72
regionalism 148–52
regulation of economy 6, 9–10, 20, 67, 70
 of finance 7
 of industries 25, 142, 163–4
Rengo [Japan Trade Union Congress] 34, 37, 40
rice import liberalisation 1, 6, 105
Russia 23

Sagawa Express 32–5
Sagawa scandal 34, 36, 40–1, 54, 60
Saito, Eishiro 37–8, 117, 119
Saito, Jiro 78
Saito, Yutaka 118–19
Sakamoto, Harumi 132
Sakurada, Takeshi 26–7
Samuels, Richard 9, 69
Sankei Shimbun 26
Sanwa 72, 116, 137–8
Sasaki, Tadashi 130–1
Sato, Eisaku 26–8, 50–1, 82, 138, 153
Sato, Tatsuo 106
scandals *see* corruption
SCAP *see* Allied Powers
Schwartz, Frank 76
Seibu Department Stores 132
Seibu Railroad 38, 156
Seiji Kaikaku Suishin Kyogikai [Political Reform Promotion Association] 40

seisaku sho [policy business] 11, 19, 31, 35, 38, 110
seisho [political business] 11, 19–21, 24, 32, 35–6, 38
Seiyukai [Association of Political Friends] 22
Sekimoto, Hisashiro 119, 153
semi-governmental organisations 130
seniority 5, 12, 84
Shibusawa, Eiichi 124
Shimokobe, Atsushi 129
Shinto, Hisashi 33
Showa Denko 49
Social Democratic Party 57, 142
 see also Japan Socialist Party
Sogo 58
sokaiya 53, 161
Sony 32, 58, 121–3, 140
state intervention 7
Sumitomo 25, 118, 122, 137–8, 152
Sumitomo Chemical Industries 119, 121
Sumitomo Electronics 40
Suntory 58
Suzuki 58
Suzuki, Toshifumi 121

Taisei Construction 58–9
Taiwan 138
Takahashi, Harunori 90
Takaishi, Kunio 33
Takeda, Yutaka 119
Takeshita, Noboru 33–5, 37, 61, 82, 89, 105, 129
Takeshita (Noboru) faction 88, 143
Tanaka, Kakuei 24, 26–9, 31, 51–2, 61, 108, 129
Tanaka (Kakuei) faction 38, 51–2, 86–8, 104, 143
Tanaka style politics 88
Taya, Hiroaki 90
Toda Construction 58–9
Tokugawa regime 4, 21, 47, 151

Tokyo Electric Power 29, 54, 117–18, 121–3, 129, 155
Tokyu (Tokyo Kyuko) 127, 156
Toray 121–2
Toshiba 29, 58, 118, 120, 141
Toyo Construction 58
Toyota 37, 39, 58–9, 118–19, 122, 140, 157
Toyota, Eiji 119
Toyota, Shoichiro 37, 117–20, 132
Tsuji, Yoshifumi 121–2
Tsutsumi, Yoshiaki 38

Uejima, Shigeji 121
Uemura, Kogoro 27, 117–18, 166
UK 4, 7, 23, 48, 107, 115
urbanisation 50
Uriu, Robert 9, 68
USA 4, 6–8, 23, 39, 48, 68, 107, 125, 132
    friction with 6, 30, 40, 144
Ushio, Haruo 131
Ushio Electronics 131
Usui, Nobuaki 100

Vogel, Steven 68, 97

Wakui, Yoji 100
Watanabe, Hiroyasu 34
Watanabe, Tomoyoshi 106
Watanabe, Yoshimi 106
Weiss, Linda 7
Welfare Ministry 93
Wilson, Graham 19

yakuza 23, 35, 89, 160–1
Yamaguchi, Nobuo 128
Yamaguchi, Toshio 90
Yamaichi securities 8, 26, 28
Yamashita, Ganri 38
Yamazaki, Taku 60
Yamazaki (Taku) faction 61, 104, 106
Yanaga, Chitoshi 2
Yasuda 21
Yosano, Kaoru 105
Yoshida, Shigeru 50

zaibatsu 5, 21, 23, 26, 48, 114, 117, 122, 129, 136–7
    dissolution of 5, 23, 137
zaikai [Japanese business world] 1
Zenekon [General Federation of Construction Companies] 41, 143
zoku [policy tribes] 12, 81, 83–7, 91–2, 100, 103–10, 140, 142–3, 153, 163, 165